Six Pillars From Ephesians

Intimacy With God

T.D. JAKES

SIX PILLARS FROM EPHESIANS

Intimacy With God

THE SPIRITUAL WORSHIP OF THE BELIEVER

BETHANYHOUSE

MINNEAPOLIS, MINNESOTA

Published by Bethany House Publishers
11400 Hampshire Avenue South
Bloomington, Minnesota 55438
www.bethanyhouse.com

Bethany House Publishers is a Division of Baker Book House
Company, Grand Rapids, Michigan.

Printed in the United States of America.

Library of Congress Cataloging-in-Publication Data

Jakes, T. D.
    Intimacy with God : the spiritual worship of the believer /
by T. D. Jakes.
        p. cm.– (Six pillars from Ephesians ; v. 3)
Includes bibliographical references.
Originally published: Tulsa, Okla. : Albury Pub., c1999. (Jakes,
T. D. Six pillars from Ephesians ; v. 3)
    ISBN 0-7642-2841-2 (pbk.)
    1. Bible. N.T. Ephesians–Criticism, interpretation, etc. 2.
Spiritual life– Christianity. I. Title.
    BS2695.52.J35 2003
    227'.506–dc22   2003014738

CONTENTS

INTIMACY WITH GOD
THE SPIRITUAL WORSHIP
OF THE BELIEVER

INTRODUCTION

When we speak of worship, what usually comes to mind is the segment of our church services when the congregation sings songs of praise and worship to the Lord. We begin with praise, the faster and louder songs that move to a strong beat and cause us to jump and shout and dance with joy. During praise, while we are (sometimes wildly) hopping around and rejoicing, our focus is on everything God has done, is doing, and will do for us. Then there comes a point in the singing when the Spirit of God moves us to slow down, get softer, and focus our attention entirely upon Jesus. Now we leave all temporal things behind, enter into the Holy of Holies in the heavenlies, bow our hearts to the ground, and see and hear only Him. We are consumed by our Lord and Savior, worshipping Him with our whole being.

When we speak of worship in this way, it is a most sacred experience, and the beautiful thing is, we can have this experience anywhere and at any time. We do not have to wait till Sunday morning, which leads to my main point. As exhilarating, burden-lifting, and life-transforming as worship in our services can be, this is only a part of the meaning of worship for the believer. Worship comprises the very essence and foundation of our life in Christ. Worship is the complete consecration of our lives to God. It is the attitude we walk in, speak from, and meditate in at all times. Our life is completely and totally His.

The attitude and place of worship we walk in each day is the classroom of the Holy Spirit. The more we cultivate and develop a worshipful manner of life, the more He can teach us about God, His thoughts, and His ways. As we grow up in God, we know more. We see more. We understand more. And we *surrender* more!

Remaining faithful to God's Word and following the leading of the Holy Spirit means we give up this idol and turn over that obsession, put off the old man's sinful thinking and habits, and crucify our flesh again and again. We renew our minds and cast down every vain imagination and lie of the enemy. We cultivate and immerse ourselves in a life of worship unto our God.

Through this continuous purification and progressive sanctification, we have more and more capacity to love, to be thankful, to step out in faith and power, and to worship our Creator with our whole heart. More than that, we have the maturity to commune and communicate with Him on a higher level. As mankind, we are restored to the place Adam and Eve enjoyed as they walked and talked with Him in the Garden of Eden.

Worship is falling down before the Lord in complete submission and humility *on the inside at all times,* making ourselves totally available to whatever He would have us say or do. It is inviting the Holy Spirit to transform us and make us into the fullness of the image of Jesus Christ. It is yielding all that we have and all that we are to the refining power of God so that He might use us and flow through us to bless others. Worship is giving to the Lord all of the honor and glory due His name twenty-four hours a day.

Worship expands our intimate knowledge of our Creator and deepens our faith in Him. And our worship is never ending. What we do in worship on earth today is only a prelude to what we will be doing throughout eternity. In this world, we worship as once-lost creatures who now bow before the God who has found them, quickened them, and made them alive forever.

We can never fully comprehend all that God is, but the more we worship Him, and the more we love and understand His thoughts and ways, the more we love to worship Him with every breath of our lives. With each new revelation about our incredible God, the richer and deeper and higher our worship becomes. To know Him is to worship Him. When we truly know Him, we can't help but worship Him. He is our all in all, our beginning and ending. He is Alpha and Omega. He is Lord of all. He is King of Kings. In Him we live and move and have our being!

When we consider worship in light of the book of Ephesians, we see clearly why the apostle Paul waits until the first verse of the third chapter to declare that he is nothing more than a prisoner of Jesus Christ. Worshippers are different from praisers, because they have stepped beyond thanking God for altering their *conditions* to worshipping Him for their *position* as His children. They love Him for who He is, and they are forever humbled by whom He has made them to be.

In *Loved By God,* we explored the first chapter of Ephesians, which describes in detail the incomprehensible reality of who God is and all He accomplished in His redemptive work through Jesus Christ. In *Experiencing Jesus,* we dug into the second

8

chapter of Ephesians, where God mercifully quickens us with Christ, raises and seats us together with Him and with each other, and makes us a holy temple in which He dwells forever. By chapter three, Paul falls upon his face and cries, "I am undone by the revelation of my Creator and all He has done for me. I am nothing but a prisoner of the Lord Jesus Christ! All I can do is worship Him!"

You see, Paul was not forced or made to be a prisoner of Jesus Christ. He *chose* to be His prisoner. Many believers choose to allow Jesus to save them and heal them and set them free, but few believers choose to become His prisoners. The Greek word Paul used here was *desmios*, which can mean not only to be held captive, but to be bound. Paul not only allowed the Lord Jesus Christ to take him captive when he was saved on the road to Damascus, but he bound himself to Jesus in his daily life.

To Paul, worship was not something he did occasionally as a ritual or special event; it was something he did continually. Following his example, worship of our God must not be something we do with one aspect of our being, such as our voice; it is something we must do with all that we are. Worship of our God is not accomplished in services from time to time; *worship is our service.* Nor is worship something we do only when we are happy and blessed. We worship God in all situations and circumstances.

Worship flows from our spirit in power, infuses our soul with understanding, gives divine expression to our bodies, and causes illumination of our countenance. Believers in Christ Jesus don't have to stop to think about worship. We don't say, "I think I'll pause to worship God now." No — we *live* in a state of worship and give expression to worship as our first response, our first thought, our first emotion, and our first action.

Worship of our God is our highest calling, our deepest walk, and our greatest joy. Worship brings *Intimacy With God.*

1

FOR THIS CAUSE

For this cause I Paul, the prisoner of Jesus Christ for you Gentiles.

EPHESIANS 3:1

The apostle Paul was a man of purpose. He understood who he was in Christ and he knew his role in God's plan for the Church. Much can be said about him, but I believe it is important to know three things about his former life, as Saul of Tarsus, which formed his character and ultimately produced a life which graphically and dynamically expressed complete surrender to Jesus Christ — the epitome of worship.

First, Saul of Tarsus was an extremely intelligent man. He had the ability and intellect to readily adapt himself to whatever audience he happened to be addressing or company he was keeping. He knew enough about the Greek culture to preach effectively to the Greeks. As a Roman citizen, he was thoroughly familiar with the Roman way of life. Yet he knew the Scriptures inside and out and could talk at ease on any scriptural matter with the Jews. He was affluent, influential, well-known, and highly respected by all of the scholars and theologians of his day — until he became Paul, the Christian!

You must understand that the Gentile intellectuals and highly religious Jews of that time considered Christians insane. After all, they believed in a God who had become a man, died, and then risen from the dead. They believed in a Messiah whom most of Israel had rejected. It was acceptable for a rough, superstitious fisherman like Peter to preach Christ, but not Paul the scholar! Christianity was associated with those who were unlearned and not very religious. Once Paul became a Christian, he was an oxymoron. He was an "intelligent Christian." He didn't fit the mold. He was highly educated and had always been zealously religious. He had an impeccable heritage that should have never led to his conversion to this ludicrous worship of a Jew by the name of Jesus of Nazareth.

Second, Saul of Tarsus was a truly multicultural person. We hear a great deal today about multicultural churches, but let me assure you of this: You cannot have a multicultural church just by mixing cultures and races together. The people in the church must be multicultural in their *thinking*. To be multicultural is to be able to walk in another person's culture without trying to alter it. It is to have an appreciation for diversity. Because Saul was well-traveled, well-read, and spoke several languages, he was as at ease and accepted among the intelligentsia of Rome as he was among the Pharisees of Jerusalem. This made him truly multicultural. By the time he was converted, he was well aware of the traditions and thinking of all the people to whom he would minister.

Third, Saul of Tarsus had the best of ancestry and heritage. If any Jew had confidence and pride in his natural lineage and upbringing, it was Saul of Tarsus. Let's read the apostle Paul's own description of himself:

> **T**hough I might also have confidence in the flesh. If any other man thinketh that he hath whereof he might trust in the flesh, I more:
>
> Circumcised the eighth day, of the stock of Israel, of the tribe of Benjamin, an Hebrew of the Hebrews; as touching the law, a Pharisee;
>
> Concerning zeal, persecuting the church; touching the righteousness which is in the law, blameless.
>
> PHILIPPIANS 3:4-6

You would think Saul's intelligence, his multicultural acumen, and the high regard he carried as a Jew would never allow him to bow before Jesus Christ, and yet he did. What was it that brought him to the place where his paramount objective in life was to embrace this Jesus of Nazareth as

Messiah and to reveal Him to others in all of His splendor? How did God strip Saul of Tarsus of all reliance upon his brilliant mind, his multicultural identity, and his heritage as a Roman citizen and a righteous Jew? He made him a prisoner.

THE PRISONER

And as he journeyed, he came near Damascus: and suddenly there shined round about him a light from heaven:

And he fell to the earth, and heard a voice saying unto him, Saul, Saul, why persecutest thou me?

And he said, Who art thou, Lord? And the Lord said, I am Jesus whom thou persecutest: it is hard for thee to kick against the pricks.

ACTS 9:3-5

Saul of Tarsus was on his way to the city of Damascus in Syria to kill any believers he could find there when he ran into Jesus of Nazareth — the very Jesus he hated. In one statement, Jesus completely turned the tables on Paul and he was locked up forever as a prisoner in His service. He declared to Paul that by persecuting Him and His followers, he was fighting God and literally kicking "against the pricks."

In the Middle East in that time, oxen were controlled by farmers who used a sharp instrument to goad or prod them into motion in the right direction. Pens in which oxen were kept were lined with these "pricks" to keep the oxen in place, as moving against them would cause the oxen great pain. By using this illustration, we can see that there was no enticement in the Lord's call on Saul's life. He didn't tease him or coax him with blessing plans. He didn't say, "I'm going to make you wealthy" or "I'm going to make you famous and important." He simply said, "Saul, you are completely out of the will of God. You are literally fighting Me like a rebellious, stubborn ox who is kicking against the pricks."

Saul responded in an instant and humbled himself. Trembling there on the ground before the Lord, he said, "What wilt thou have me to do?" (Acts 9:6). Later, in Damascus, the Lord showed him what he was going to suffer for the Gospel. The message was direct: "You are my chosen vessel, and you will suffer many things for this cause I give you." Did Saul take three days to consider the matter? No, he went immediately to the believers there and presented himself for service. No longer was he the dreaded and cruel Saul of Tarsus, but Paul, the prisoner of Jesus Christ.

The apostle Paul worshipped Jesus with a total abandonment of all his natural credentials and lived in complete compliance to the Holy Spirit. When he desired to travel to certain cities and he felt the Holy Spirit constraining him, he didn't go. When others warned him not to go certain places and he felt the Holy Spirit compelling him, he went, regardless of threats to his life. He identified himself simply as "the prisoner of Jesus Christ."

To be a powerful, effective Christian means that you must be a prisoner, a slave to Jesus Christ. When God says to do something, you do it, with no regard for what people may think about you or say about you. You obey Him regardless of how you feel at any given moment or about any given thing. To be a prisoner of Jesus Christ is to be chained to Him, which means you automatically go where He goes, say what He says, and do what He does. It is to comply with His will fully and to allow the Word of God and the leading of the Holy Spirit to rule your heart and mind.

The time has come when we must stop confusing preachers with politicians. Shaking hands and kissing babies is not what being a preacher is all about! Being a preacher is solely about obedience to God and saying what God wants said. And this applies to all believers! Whether we are clergy or laity, full-time or part-time, on staff or a volunteer — we are all ministers and prisoners of Jesus Christ.

Paul knew that eventually he was going to be killed for the Gospel he preached. Nevertheless, he preached it — passionately and joyfully. How many Christians today would be willing to go to a city and preach the Gospel if they knew the result of their obedience could be imprisonment or death? I suspect very few. And yet that attitude and lifestyle of worship is what is required of us if we are going to be useful to God as witnesses of the Gospel. *All of us may not have to die for Christ in the physical sense, but we all must die to self in the spiritual sense.*

Those who are prisoners of Jesus Christ know that the message they proclaim is far more important than themselves as a messenger. The message takes center stage. The messenger is just a backdrop on which the message has been painted with brokenness and pain, surrender and submission, and utter joy of their salvation. Prisoners of Jesus Christ have yielded fully to God's call on their lives and continually put off the world, their flesh, and the devil in their daily lives.

Just before he was beheaded on the Appian Way, Paul wrote to Timothy from his prison cell in Rome, "I have finished my course. I have kept the faith" (2 Timothy 4:7). He knew the time of his departure was at hand. From the first moment on the Damascus road to a prison cell in Rome, Paul was the prisoner of Jesus Christ. And the question he asked the moment he received Jesus Christ was the question of his heart for every moment thereafter: "What wilt thou have me to do?"

WHAT WILT THOU HAVE ME TO DO?

There was nothing in Paul's career as a minister of the Gospel that was prestigious. Although he was equipped by education and experience to debate the law with the most intellectual Jewish scholars in Israel, to whom did the Lord send Paul?

For this cause I Paul, the prisoner of Jesus Christ for you Gentiles.

EPHESIANS 3:1

Not only was Paul the prisoner of Jesus Christ, but God locked him up with the idolatrous, whoremongering, homosexual-practicing Gentiles! If being knocked off his horse by a bolt of lightning didn't shake Paul up, this should have. This was the ultimate in public humiliation for a Jew with his background and abilities.

Paul was not sent first to the pristine halls of the temple in Jerusalem to proclaim the name of the risen Messiah. Nor was he sent first and foremost to the courts of kings and noblemen to preach Jesus Christ. No — God gave Paul the primary objective to reach the unclean, immoral, idol-worshippers of the Roman Empire. And one of the sleaziest cities in the world was Ephesus, a city filled with debauchery, polygamy, incest, orgies, and degradation, where men were lovers of themselves and where pride reigned supreme. Paul was directed to preach the Gospel and teach the mysteries of Christ Jesus to people he probably wouldn't even have spoken to before he received Jesus.

Could it be that the following passage in Ephesians, chapter 2, was not merely Paul's knowledge of the truth about Jew and Gentile coming together as one in Christ Jesus, but literally born from his spirit as he struggled with and conquered the issue himself?

> **W**herefore remember, that ye being in time past Gentiles in the flesh, who are called Uncircumcision by that which is called the Circumcision in the flesh made by hands;
>
> That at that time ye were without Christ, being aliens from the commonwealth of Israel, and strangers from the covenants of promise, having no hope, and without God in the world:
>
> But now in Christ Jesus ye who sometimes were far off are made nigh by the blood of Christ.
>
> For he is our peace, who hath made both one, and hath broken down the middle wall of partition between us;
>
> Having abolished in his flesh the enmity, even the law of commandments contained in ordinances; for to make in himself of twain one new man, so making peace;

And that he might reconcile both unto God in one body by the cross, having slain the enmity thereby:

And came and preached peace to you which were afar off, and to them that were nigh.

EPHESIANS 2:11-17

Paul had a revelation from God about the Gentiles and the Church, and without that revelation, he would never have been able to fulfill his calling. God had revealed to him the mystery of the Church, and he was consumed with it. He became the greatest expositor of God's blueprint for the Church who has ever lived. If you pulled all of his epistles out of the New Testament, the Church would be lost, because Paul defines and articulates the functioning of the New Testament Church. Without the apostle Paul, we never would have understood how we were to function as the literal body of Christ.

For example, Jesus empowered the Church by giving us the Holy Spirit at Pentecost, but in his epistles, Paul enumerates specifically and thoroughly how we are to operate in the power of the Holy Spirit as individuals and as a corporate body. First Corinthians, chapters 12-14, in particular call the local church body and the individual believer to a place of love, order, and integrity with regard to moving in the supernatural power of God.

You can always tell when a local church body is operating in the power of God but has not studied the Word of God, specifically the New Testament epistles, and followed the New Testament pattern and order. They are like powerful ships with no rudder. They pump out steam and their smoke-stacks are blowing great gusts, but they sail in circles — never going anywhere — never growing up and maturing in the operation of God's power.

Some of the foundational principles Paul teaches the Church about flowing gracefully in the power of the Holy Spirit are:

- We are all members of one body, and there are different administrations, but we are of one Spirit, and each member is equally vital.
- Prophesy one by one, not everyone at the same time! And if you have a tongue for the church body, it should be interpreted.
- The gifts of the Spirit are given as the Holy Spirit wills.

Paul's mandate from God was to bring the revelation of Jesus Christ to the Gentiles and then bring understanding, order, and truth to the churches they formed. To accomplish this, he traveled extensively and wrote prolifically. The Church must be forever indebted to his faithfulness to carry out his mission, for the epistles of Paul lay

21

the foundation for who we are and how we are to function as the body of Christ.

PAUL'S CHARGE TO
OUR GENERATION

In his epistles, Paul unveils before our eyes God's glorious Church. Pulling away the curtain of ignorance and darkness, he reveals to believers what the Church really is and how the body of Christ is ordained by God to operate in this earth. Our generation desperately needs to embrace this heavenly understanding and vision of who we are as the Church, because the enemy is sending every deception and evil work against us to destroy that understanding and neutralize our vision. We must be defined by God's Word and led by the Holy Spirit — nothing more and nothing less.

If we don't understand what the Church is and ignore the New Testament epistles, humanism will pass for the Church, psychic readers will pass for prophets, mind-power and familiar spirits will pass for the Holy Spirit, positive thinking will pass for faith, and Satan's supernatural ability will pass for God's presence and power. The glory of God will be replaced with Satan's "aura." And his pale, flimsy, ultimately life-destroying spiritism will deceive many to turn from the true abundant life offered through Jesus Christ.

Remember what Paul's final warning to the Ephesian leaders was before he left them in Acts 21? The wolves are coming! Don't be deceived! Don't let anyone or anything redefine who we are in the kingdom of God. Being a worshipper is not just singing and jumping and shouting with reckless abandon at meetings. Being a worshipper is submitting fully to the Word of God and the Spirit of God at all times. Only the true worshipper will spot the wolves and have the power to dispel them. Only the true worshipper will grow up into the image of Jesus Christ.

As the Church, we are this unique, new thing. We are the only ones on the planet who are spiritually born into this body through the death, burial, and resurrection of our Savior God, Christ Jesus. As individuals, our past is buried and we have newness of life. As a corporate body, we are an awesome entity without precedent. No carnal, unregenerated mind can comprehend us because we are *the mystery.*

2

THE MYSTERY

Not too long ago, there were articles in the paper reporting statements made by a certain denomination about marriage, specifically a wife's submission to her husband and her role in the family. Immediately, secular minds began arguing against that statement, and leaders of the Church began to "dialogue" with them. Suddenly we heard statements from Church leaders like, "No, that's not what we really meant. What we really meant was..."

> **B**ut the natural man receiveth not the things of the Spirit of God: for they are foolishness unto him: neither can he know them, because they are spiritually discerned.
>
> 1 CORINTHIANS 2:14

If we are not careful, we are going to allow unconverted human minds to redefine the New Testament Church God has established. If the natural mind does not comprehend the things of the Spirit of God, and the things of the Spirit include divine understanding of God's Word, why is the Church entering into this fruitless biblical debate with unbelievers? Most importantly, why are we backing down from God's Word? The Church must come to grips with the reality that the world will never accept us. We are a mystery!

There are two realities we must understand as the Church. First, we need to continue preaching the Gospel without apology and without shame, and if unbelievers reject Jesus Christ and call us crazy, then so be it. Second, we need to face the fact that the epistles were not written to the unbeliever, but to the believer. Submission of a wife to a husband in the godly, righteous, holy sense of the New Testament is not a concept the worldly mind can grasp. Unbelievers are supposed to think these teachings are ridiculous! They have no spiritual capacity to receive them, and Paul exhorts us that these truths are "foolishness" to them. The unregenerated person cannot comprehend that submission can bring freedom and joy, because this is "spiritually discerned," and they are spiritually dead.

Paul's letters were written specifically to us, this new, unique mystery called the Church. We are the ones who are filled with God's Spirit, the Teacher who gives illumination, divine empowerment, and comfort. With the Holy Spirit living inside us, we are alive to God, have the spiritual capacity to comprehend Paul's letters and teachings, and thus possess the grace to obey the Word of God. It takes the Holy Spirit in us to be able to live the life of a worshipper of Jesus Christ. Paul understood this.

MADE KNOWN BY REVELATION

> For this cause I Paul, the prisoner of Jesus Christ for you Gentiles,
> If ye have heard of the dispensation of the grace of God which is given me to you-ward.
>
> EPHESIANS 3:1-2

After expounding on the wealth and workmanship of God in chapters 1 and 2, Paul finally gets around to explaining his credentials to the Ephesians and the Church at large in chapter 3. In verse 1 he declares that he is a prisoner of Jesus Christ sent to the Gentiles. Then in verse 2 he begins to talk about the message God has given him to deliver, which he first refers to as "the dispensation of the grace of God."

Now, the word "dispensation" used here does not mean a period of time as is so often thought by believers today. It is translated from the Greek word *oikonomia*, which means "administration" or the management or oversight of something. It describes the work of a servant who has been given

27

considerable responsibility over his master's household. So Paul is saying that the responsibility or oversight of the doctrine of the grace of God has been given to him to deliver to the Gentiles. Paul then goes on in verse 3 to explain how he received this mandate:

> **How** that by revelation he made known unto me the mystery; (as I wrote afore in few words,
> Whereby, when ye read, ye may understand my knowledge in the mystery of Christ)
> Which in other ages was not made known unto the sons of men, as it is now revealed unto his holy apostles and prophets by the Spirit;
> That the Gentiles should be fellowheirs, and of the same body, and partakers of his promise in Christ by the gospel.
>
> EPHESIANS 3:3-6

It was by revelation, the word *apokalupsis*, that Paul received the understanding of the mystery. *Apokalupsis* means an unveiling, a revealing. In the same way God tore the veil of the Temple when Jesus died on the cross to reveal the Holy of Holies, He pulled aside the curtain of darkness and ignorance that had hidden the mystery of the Church for ages past and revealed the truth to Paul and to others.

The mystery, or *musterion*, literally means something we cannot possibly know without God telling us, something we cannot possibly see without God showing us. God has set this whole thing up so that we cannot truly know who we are and how we are to operate except by coming to Him and hearing it straight from Him. It is imperative for us to fellowship with the Father to understand Him, to understand ourselves, and to comprehend His plan for us. Without intimacy with Him, we are clueless!

Paul received the revelation of the mystery directly from God and relates that revelation to us in his New Testament epistles, but we must then open our hearts in faith toward God and receive His Word directly from Him — just like Paul did. It is only by divine revelation that all God has for us is made known to us.

The very creation of the Church and workmanship of God in the Church baffles the natural mind. How can anyone be born *again?* How can a believer be totally transformed by the renewing of their mind to God's Word, then grow into the full stature of Christ Jesus? We cannot fathom the mystery of godliness and holiness and perfection in Christ without operating from our spirit. We must forsake the vain reasonings of our natural mind and dive fully into the revelation flowing from the mind of Christ within us.

A mystery is also something that, on the surface, is not only baffling but which may appear to be ridiculously confusing. As I mentioned before, the entire concept of the Church is just that to the unbeliever. Unbelievers cannot begin to understand how God could create the Church and do so through crucifixion on a Roman cross and resurrection from a Jewish tomb.

And talk about ridiculous, from the Jewish perspective, just what would you think if one of your distant cousins stood up in the synagogue one day and declared that he was the Messiah. Worse yet, later he taught that he would die, and like a seed planted in the ground, rise again bringing a mighty harvest with him? You would say just what they did, "Isn't this Jesus, the carpenter's son? What is he thinking?!!!" The Jews weren't waiting for a Messiah who would be born in a manger and wrapped in swaddling clothes. They certainly weren't looking for someone who came out of Nazareth, the town where Jesus was raised. (They didn't remember that he was born in Bethlehem in accordance with Old Testament prophecy about the Messiah.)

The Jews of that time were expecting a noble king to come riding on a white horse and secure their independence from Roman rule. But this Jesus of Nazareth — "Can any good thing come out of Nazareth?" — was an embarrassment to the Jews, who saw Him as a rabble-rouser and troublemaker. He could bring great harm to them by aggravating Rome. If He did not have the supernatural power to defeat Rome, He should just be quiet and stop agitating everyone. Nothing Jesus did made sense to them, and yet He was amassing an incredibly large following. Finally the only thing that made sense to them was to cry, "Crucify Him. Get Him out of the way!"

Saul of Tarsus was one of those who held this opinion. He had actually been one of the leaders who believed that all Christians should be eliminated. He held the coats of those who stoned Stephen in Acts 7:58-60. And now here we are reading the apostle Paul's letter to the Gentile Ephesians, declaring the very thing he had once considered to be not only ridiculous but dangerous!

What made the difference in Paul's life? Revelation. On the road to Damascus, his natural eyes were blinded while his spiritual eyes were opened. Paul's spirit had been illuminated by the truth concerning the grace of God, and this revelation caused a complete conversion in his life.

THE LEAST OF ALL SAINTS

Can you imagine God whispering in your ear the meaning of a mystery, and then when you proclaim that meaning, everybody thinks you're crazy? That's the situation in which Paul found himself. People generally thought he had lost his mind when it came to talking about a crucified Messiah and a resurrected Lord. Moreover, the people who knew Jesus best — the apostles — also questioned Paul because of his past. As a result, Paul was often an isolated and controversial figure in the early Church. He was called by God to preach something for which he had very little Old Testament validation. Because the Church was a mystery from ages past, God had only hinted about its existence in the Old Testament.

Let's look at some of the aspects of the mystery of the Church which Paul brought to us by way of revelation from the Holy Spirit. The life of Jesus Christ Himself was a mystery hid in God, and something our natural mind cannot comprehend. How can a young virgin girl conceive and bear a child and still be a virgin? How can the death of one man qualify to pay for the sins of the entire human race? How can someone die, be buried, and then come back to life in an immortal, corporeal body? Who is this resurrected Lord who takes the time to remove His grave clothes and leave them neatly folded in the tomb?

So here was Paul, sent to the Gentiles to preach something no one had ever heard before, including the Jews. To make matters worse, there was very little Old Testament Scripture to confirm what he was teaching. Yet there can be no doubt that Paul understood and skillfully and powerfully delivered the message of the mystery, the revelation of the Church, the body of Jesus Christ. And how did he do that?

> **W**hereof I was made a minister, according to the gift of the grace of God given unto me by the effectual working of his power.
> Unto me, who am less than the least of all saints, is this grace given, that I should preach among the Gentiles the unsearchable riches of Christ.
>
> EPHESIANS 3:7-8

Paul received the revelation of the mystery from God and delivered that message to the Gentiles the same way he received salvation: by grace, through faith. His faith and trust in God opened his heart to receive the vision of this unique new entity called the Church. Then, filled with a passion to see this glorious Church raised up, he marched out to proclaim it to the world and become one of God's master carpenters. In verse 7, Paul is referring distinctly to the moment when he was saved on the road to Damascus when he says, "Whereof I was made a minister...by the effectual working of his power." It was the grace of God that saved him, it was the grace of God that gave him his calling, and it was the grace of God that enabled him to fulfill his calling.

Then Paul continues by calling himself "the least of all saints." He is saying, "Yes, I have been given this awesome responsibility to bring the revelation of the mystery, the understanding of who and what the Church is, to you Gentiles. But just in case you start thinking I'm so much smarter and greater than you are, I want you to know that I received this call and this revelation the same way you did: by grace, through faith. And the supernatural power that is working in me, 'the effectual working of his power,' is in you too!"

> *For I am the least of the apostles, that am not meet to be called an apostle, because I persecuted the church of God.*
>
> 1 CORINTHIANS 15:9

> *This is a faithful saying, and worthy of all acceptation, that Christ Jesus came into the world to save sinners, of whom I am chief.*
>
> 1 TIMOTHY 1:15

There is no arrogance left in Paul as he writes to the Ephesians. He genuinely regards himself as the "least" among the saints. After his conversion on the road to Damascus, he was convicted that he was the chiefest of sinners and not worthy to be called an apostle because, as Saul of Tarsus, he had persecuted and murdered Christians with zeal and satisfaction. I believe the reason Paul possibly understood and appreciated the message of God's grace more than any other believer of his time was because he considered himself completely unworthy of God's mercy and grace. Everything in his being cried out in sheer awe and gratitude that Jesus even saved him, let alone made him a minister of the Gospel.

Today, we have far too many Christians who think that they did God a favor by allowing Him into their lives. They may not say it outright, but their attitude and behavior often depict:

- "I'm an executive. I have a master's degree. I could be doing something else and making a lot more money, but I decided to make my services available to the church."
- "I'm a psalmist. I could be recording secular music. I used to have contracts in the world, but I've decided to do this benefit for the church."
- "I hadn't intended to come to church today, but it's a good thing I did, because otherwise I wouldn't have been here to prophesy."

We don't see many who are willing to proclaim themselves to be the "least" among the saints! But this spirit of genuine humility is required if we are to truly worship God and fulfill His plan. If we don't have an *attitude* of being least among the saints, we are never going to have the *altitude* of being great in the kingdom of God. Those who wonder why people aren't healed when their shadow falls upon the sick folk lying in the marketplace need to check their attitude. Those who wonder why the power of God doesn't seem to be moving through them so that souls are saved need to check their attitude. Those who wonder why demons don't flee when they attempt to cast them out need to check their attitude.

Paul's attitude of humility was the key to his receiving the revelation of the Church. His very life illustrated the essence of the message he carried: the grace of God was so limitless that He offered salvation even to His worst enemy, Saul of Tarsus. The Christian killer became a Christian.

A HUMBLING TRUTH

Which in other ages was not made known unto the sons of men, as it is now revealed unto his holy apostles and prophets by the Spirit;

That the Gentiles should be fellowheirs, and of the same body, and partakers of his promise in Christ by the gospel.

EPHESIANS 3:5-6

Few of us today can begin to comprehend the intense hatred that the Jews had for Gentiles in the time of Paul. If a Gentile sat at the table with a Jew, the Jew would break his plate, get up, and leave. Even the idea of breaking bread with a Gentile was mind-boggling to a Jew. So intense was the dividing line between Jew and Gentile, we witnessed Jesus' refusal at first to even speak with the Syrophoenician woman in Mark 7:24-30. Yet now Paul is asking Jews and Gentiles to sit down at the same communion table and to partake of the Bread of Life, Jesus Christ. Can you see the incredible act of humility it took for Paul to carry out his calling?

Jesus told a parable which foretold how this scenario would unfold.

> **A** certain man made a great supper, and bade many:
>
> And sent his servant at supper time to say to them that were bidden, Come; for all things are now ready.
>
> And they all with one consent began to make excuse. The first said unto him, I have bought a piece of ground, and I must needs go and see it: I pray thee have me excused.
>
> And another said, I have bought five yoke of oxen, and I go to prove them: I pray thee have me excused.
>
> And another said, I have married a wife, and therefore I cannot come.
>
> So that servant came, and shewed his lord these things. Then the master of the house being angry said to his servant, Go out quickly into the streets and lanes

of the city, and bring in hither the poor, and the maimed, and the halt, and the blind.

And the servant said, Lord, it is done as thou hast commanded, and yet there is room.

And the lord said unto the servant, Go out into the highways and hedges, and compel them to come in, that my house may be filled.

For I say unto you, That none of those men which were bidden shall taste of my supper.

LUKE 14:16-24

The first call of God was to Israel — an elect group, God's chosen — by Jesus Himself during His earthly ministry. The invitation was as old as Abraham, an invitation to "come and dine." But when God served the Bread of Life and sat Him down at the table, the nation of Israel made excuses about why they could not partake, and they walked away.

The second call was to the Gentiles — the halt, lame, deaf, dumb, and blind. The Master was saying, "Let anybody come to the table." The *anybody* includes US! All of us unclean, uncircumcised Gentiles came to the Master's house to partake of a formal, sit-down dinner with white linen. The Church is a "spread" that was prepared for aristocrats and eaten by common folk like us. This is where Paul entered, center stage, to proclaim the mystery of the Church, which would be predominantly Gentiles.

The third call is the challenge for the end of the age, because there is still room at the Master's table for all those who will come. And since no man knows the day or the hour, we are all a part of this call. We are to go and compel the final harvest to come in before the entrance is closed to the Master's house. What a marvelous grace! What a privilege is ours!

It's little wonder the Jews in Paul's time didn't know what to think. God had broken all protocol in saving the Gentiles. He had broken the generations-old "religious etiquette" in calling for these formerly heathen believers to be filled with His Holy Spirit. A humbling message, to be sure, for a Jew with the heritage and background of Saul of Tarsus! But Paul the apostle realized that he was one of the Master's servants going into the highways and byways, compelling guests to come to the table and share in communion with the Lord and with one another. He knew the Gentiles, who once would never have been allowed near the holy things of Israel, were now being invited by the Holy One of Israel to have intimate fellowship with Him.

Delivering the mystery of the Church was a monumental responsibility and all-consuming task. We are a spiritual body born from God through the shed blood of Jesus Christ. We are the coming together of Gentile and Jew, bond and free, male and female. We are citizens of heaven who operate on earth according to our spiritual position, transcending and overcoming our natural conditions. We are a holy nation, a peculiar people, set apart exclusively for God's use.

It was because Paul was continuously overawed by the manifold grace of God toward him that he could humbly deliver the revelation of the mystery first to the Gentiles, then to the Jew, and finally to kings. His gratitude and heart of worship toward God is what allowed and enabled him to carry out God's plan for his life. As "the least of all saints," he became great in the kingdom as the one who faithfully and powerfully proclaimed the mystery which was hid in God from the creation of the world.

3
UNSEARCHABLE RICHES

Unto me, who am less than the least of all saints, is this grace given, that I should preach among the Gentiles the unsearchable riches of Christ.

EPHESIANS 3:8

Paul was given grace by God to proclaim to the Gentiles the "unsearchable riches of Christ." "Unsearchable" is the Greek word *anexichniaston*, which literally means these riches cannot be searched out or tracked out. The contemporary meaning for the word "unsearchable" would be something that could not be explored or examined. However, here Paul invites us to do all the exploring of Christ's riches we can. Then, when we are finally exhausted from our search, we will discover that we have only begun to enjoy what He has for us. No matter how much we search and no matter how much we find in Him, we will never come to the end of His riches.

How big is the God you worship?

"Oh, He's infinite and omnipotent and awesome," you may say. But let me ask again: How big is God *to you*?

Is God big enough to meet *all* your needs?

Is God big enough to handle *all* your problems?

Is God big enough to fulfill *all* your desires?

Is He so big, you cannot even begin to comprehend how big He is?

One of the words used as a synonym for unsearchable is unfathomable, which alludes to a search mission in the open sea or ocean. When seafarers want to determine how deep the water is, they emit sounds into the water. Then they measure the time it takes to hear the sound reflected off the bottom of the ocean. The unit of measure for this sounding is called a fathom, a nautical unit of measure about six feet in length. When something is unfathomable, the thought is that the bottom of the ocean is so far down that when the sound is sent it never returns. What a powerful word picture of the full measure of Christ's riches in our lives! There is no tracking the end of them. We can spend all we want of His riches and still not put a dent in His supply.

Understanding that Christ's riches are unsearchable and unfathomable frees us from many of the hazards of riches. Normally, when people have access to riches, they remain secretive, protective of their find, and selfish. They will hire elaborate security staffs and change their daily habits in an effort to protect and hoard their wealth. Excessive wealth often destroys relationships and can cause extensive personal problems. But the riches of Christ are inexhaustible, so we are free to share them and spend them without worrying about poverty tomorrow. These riches mean we are freed from jealousy, envy, and strife. And we are free to love, to joy in our salvation, and to impart this same salvation and grace to others.

Unsearchable riches means that a person can look at Jesus Christ their entire lifetime and never discover all of His wealth and glory. The riches of Christ Jesus are unfathomable, beyond full exploration, beyond full discovery, beyond full experience, and beyond full knowing. Paul — highly educated, speaking several languages, multicultural in thought, possessing excellent communication skills — would be the first to admit, "I can't even articulate how much I've discovered in Christ."

As worshippers of God, this is great news! There is no place to go but higher and deeper in spirit and in truth. None of us is capable of fully understanding the nature of God or experiencing the full presence of God in our lives. None of us can take into ourselves all that Christ Jesus offers to us.

None of us can see fully the big picture God sees or grasp all that He is.

FELLOWSHIP OF THE MYSTERY

> **T**o make all men see what is the fellowship of the mystery, which from the beginning of the world hath been hid in God, who created all things by Jesus Christ.
>
> EPHESIANS 3:9

Now Paul gets very specific about what, exactly, the unsearchable riches of Christ are. The fellowship of the mystery, or the *oikonomia* of the *musterion* in the Greek language, uses two words we have just discussed in the previous chapter. Paul is to make all men see the administration (*oikonomia*) of that which can only be known by revelation from God (*musterion*). Literally, he is to explain to us how God brought forth and oversaw the creation of the Church and reveal the workmanship of God in the body of Christ. Then he goes on to say that this has been hid in God from the beginning of the world.

God had laid out the blueprint of His great plan from the beginning of the ages, from the very foundation of the world. He had a plan to redeem mankind, which included a special time period when predominantly Gentiles would be redeemed. We call this the Church Age. That plan was hidden

44

for thousands of years because the first stage of God's plan was to pull out the Hebrews and bring them into covenant with Him. They were the first-fruits, and the Gentiles were the latter-day harvest.

Only a few clues were given to the prophets in the Old Testament about this aspect of God's plan, but when Jesus began to preach, He made mention of the Gentiles often and demonstrated how they were redeemed by grace, through faith, just like Abraham, Isaac, and Jacob. One time, He reminded the people that in Naaman's day, all of the lepers who were in Israel died of leprosy but Naaman, who was a Gentile. He recovered from this dread disease because he sought out God's prophet Elisha and obeyed his commands, which showed his faith in God. (See Luke 4:27 and 2 Kings 5:1-14.) A Gentile succeeded where the Jews had failed because he had faith in God and obeyed His prophet's commands.

Jesus also reminded them that it was a Gentile widow of Sarepta (also called Zarephath) — a city in Sidon, a territory in what we now call Lebanon — who received a miracle of provision when she gave hospitality to the prophet Elijah and obeyed his commands, while the widows of Israel died in famine. (See Luke 4:26 and 1 Kings 17:1-16.)

Jesus even ministered to Gentiles on occasion. When a Roman centurion came to Him seeking healing for his servant, Jesus healed the man. This centurion said to Him:

> Lord, my servant lieth at home sick of the palsy, grievously tormented.
>
> And Jesus saith unto him, I will come and heal him.
>
> The centurion answered and said, Lord, I am not worthy that thou shouldest come under my roof: but speak the word only, and my servant shall be healed.
>
> For I am a man under authority, having soldiers under me: and I say to this man, Go, and he goeth; and to another, Come, and he cometh; and to my servant, Do this, and he doeth it.
>
> MATTHEW 8:6-9

Jesus marveled at this man's statement and said, "Verily I say unto you, I have not found so great faith, no, not in Israel" (Matthew 8:10). He then went on to proclaim this great word about the Gentiles:

> Many shall come from the east and west, and shall sit down with Abraham, and Isaac, and Jacob, in the kingdom of heaven.
>
> But the children of the kingdom shall be cast out into outer darkness: there shall be weeping and gnashing of teeth.
>
> MATTHEW 8:11-12

In Matthew 15:22-28 we have an account where Jesus healed the daughter of a Canaanite woman who lived in the coastal region of Sidon. She came to Jesus and said, "Have mercy on me, O Lord, thou Son of David; my daughter is grievously vexed with a devil." Jesus didn't say a word to her at first. He said, "I am not sent but unto the lost sheep of the house of Israel." But then the woman fell to the ground and began to worship Jesus, saying, "Lord, help me." It was her worship of Him which caused Jesus to continue the conversation.

Jesus said to her, "It is not proper to take the children's bread and give it to dogs." The term "dog" was how the Jews routinely referred to Gentiles, and it clearly depicts the attitude of the nation of Israel toward them. Still, the woman persisted, "You're right, Lord, but even the dogs eat the crumbs which fall from their master's table." She readily admitted that she was a Gentile dog, but she also saw the possibility that even a Gentile might be given a few of the wonderful crumbs of the Bread of Life who had been sent first to the Jews.

This Gentile woman's worship was so intense that she was unmoved by any rejection or rebuff from Jesus, so He answered her, "O woman, great is your faith! You can have exactly what you desire." The Bible says that the woman's daughter was made whole from that very moment!

A few crumbs. A few clues. A few mentions of Gentiles coming into closer relationship with God. But now Paul is telling the Ephesians that the intent of God from the beginning has been revealed fully. One of the unsearchable riches of Christ is that all men, Jew and Gentile, can be saved by simply calling upon the name of the Lord Jesus Christ. We are invited to see and to know the truth of Jesus Christ, the plan of redemption God had for us from the beginning of time, and to enjoy all of His unsearchable riches.

THE POWER OF THE WORD

And to make all men see what is the fellowship of the mystery, which from the beginning of the world hath been hid in God, who created all things by Jesus Christ.

EPHESIANS 3:9

Another unfathomable treasure we have obtained as believers is the revelation of the immeasurable power of God's Word. This revelation begins with understanding that God "created all things by Jesus Christ." Like the "fellowship of the mystery," in these few words we are presented with a truth that is foolishness to the natural mind. All of creation is the work of Jesus Christ because He is the living Word of God, and God created all things by His

Word. John the apostle began his account of the Gospel with this same truth:

> In the beginning was the Word, and the Word was with God, and the Word was God.
> The same was in the beginning with God.
> All things were made by him; and without him was not any thing made that was made.
>
> JOHN 1:1-3

> And the Word was made flesh, and dwelt among us, (and we beheld his glory, the glory as of the only begotten of the Father,) full of grace and truth.
>
> JOHN 1:14

Jesus is the Word incarnate, and God continues to create all things through His Word, Jesus Christ. As John says, "Without him was not any thing made that was made." When God spoke, it was the Word, Jesus Christ, who caused God's intent to come into being, and that is true today. When God speaks, it is the Word who causes miracles to happen, the sick to be healed, the sinners to be forgiven, the demons to flee, and the weak to be made strong.

> Through faith we understand that the worlds were framed by the word of God, so that things which are seen were not made of things which do appear.
>
> HEBREWS 11:3

God speaks from the invisible realm and the Word brings forth a visible reality. We were not a people — not a Church — until Jesus Christ spoke the intent of God into existence and said, "Let there be." The same creative Word that created light in a dark void created salvation in a heathen heart!

To those who marveled and wondered, *How can this be that God would include Gentiles in His plan?* Paul said, "It is by the same power that God created the world out of nothing. The Gentiles were brought in and the Church was born out of the mouth of God." God sends His Word and His Word causes things to come into existence that were not previously seen or known. God sent His Word in the form of flesh-and-blood humanity into this world and by Christ Jesus' life, death, and resurrection, He caused a Church to be birthed that had not existed before.

God spoke in your heart the truth of Jesus Christ, you believed in Him, and you were birthed again in your spirit.

God spoke and the Holy Spirit filled your being so that you entered a new realm of existence — you in Christ and Christ in you forever.

When God speaks, reality happens! His Word is full of grace and power, fully effectual to bring about anything He desires.

One of the main reasons we praise and worship God, one of our motivations and greatest joys, is this fact that God continues to create life and wholeness and purpose out of things that seem dead and broken and void of purpose. We are what we are today because God spoke His Word and made us and remade us and continues to remake us. Everything we need, desire, hope for, and believe for is created and will be created by the power of His Word.

Nothing is beyond the power of God, and that power is expressed and manifested through His Word. Whatever He desires to exist, He *speaks* it into existence! And we partake of the unsearchable riches of Christ when we speak and proclaim His Word in the earth today. When we think and act and speak in accordance with God's Word, all the forces of nature, every demon, and even the angels of heaven must obey because God's Word is the final authority in all matters and in all situations! Every knee must bow to the name of Jesus, who is the Living Word.

If you are grasping this truth right now, your heart is bursting and your mind is spinning and your feet are dancing! In Hebrews 1:3 we read that Jesus Christ is, even today, "upholding all things by the word of his power." When God speaks, His Word has power embedded within it to do what God sends it to do and it will sustain that work forever.

For as the rain cometh down, and the snow from heaven, and returneth not thither, but watereth the earth, and maketh it bring forth and bud, that it may give seed to the sower, and bread to the eater:

So shall my word be that goeth forth out of my mouth: it shall not return unto me void, but it shall accomplish that which I please, and it shall prosper in the thing whereto I sent it.

ISAIAH 55:10-11

When you speak what God speaks and you speak it according to His will, His Word prevails over any attack and destroys any obstacle the enemy presents you with. When you live according to God's Word and believe, all things are truly possible. Now, that is unfathomable wealth!

WE TEACH THE ANGELS

To the intent that now unto the principalities and powers in heavenly places might be known by the church the manifold wisdom of God,

According to the eternal purpose which he purposed in Christ Jesus our Lord.

EPHESIANS 3:10-11

These verses of Scripture are filled with the unsearchable riches of Christ! Paul begins with "To the intent," which literally means "I'm going to tell you why God has created the Church." And in verse 11, he says that this was an "eternal purpose" or intention. In other words, this was on God's heart and in His mind throughout eternity past and passing through all the ages of time into eternity future.

Paul goes on to say that the intention of God is to use the Church to show the principalities and powers His manifold wisdom. The Greek language used in this verse tells us clearly that the principalities and powers here are not the demonic forces of Satan roaming the earth but the angelic beings of heaven. The word "heavenly" is translated from *epouraniois*, which depicts the highest celestial realm, the third heaven, where God sits and the cherubim and seraphim reside. So God has chosen us, mortal vessels of clay, to be filled with His Spirit and His Word and to display His manifold wisdom to the angelic population of the universe!

This is a mind-blowing concept! Human believers, the body of Christ, are literally teaching and imparting revelation about the mystery of the Church and the plan of salvation to Michael and Gabriel and every angelic being of heaven. Moreover, we are revealing the "manifold wisdom of God," and the word "manifold" says a lot! This is the Greek word *polupoikilos*, and if this word were used to describe an oil painting, it would be saying that the painting was filled with a multiplicity of colors, that this particular painting would be marked by the great variety of color it contained.

First Peter 1:12 talks about how the angels stoop down with a passionate desire to understand what God has done, that the cherubim gaze continually at the mercy seat in heaven, now sprinkled with the precious, life-giving blood of Jesus Christ, wondering and pondering the intent of the Father in this great work called the redemption of mankind. Paul has placed before us the baffling and awesome truth that God is using *us* to display His untold and multifaceted wisdom in His plan of redemption and the creation of the Church, that we are teaching the angels what was in the mind and heart of God from eternity past.

For some reason, God has chosen to honor us with this awesome responsibility, and like Paul, we must humbly declare that we are the least of all saints, that we are completely unworthy of such a privilege. We are overwhelmed by the unsearchable riches of Christ. And only in this attitude of worship and humility are we able to go forth and show forth the magnificent glory of God, even unto the angels.

4

TIMING IS EVERYTHING

But he answered and said, It is written, Man shall not live by bread alone, but by every word that proceedeth out of the mouth of God.

MATTHEW 4:4

Jesus told us that our life, our deliverance, our hope, and our future are found in the words that proceed from the mouth of God. His words are the truth with which we worship Him, as we are to worship Him in spirit and in truth. And the first and final and absolute words which proceeded from the mouth of God and which form the very foundation of our lives are found in the Holy Scriptures.

OUT OF GOD'S MOUTH

God's Word is eternal, beginning in eternity past and extending to eternity future. God's Word is also absolute. Nothing can be added to it, and nothing can be subtracted from it. Jesus, as God's Word, is everlasting truth. Nothing can be subtracted from His life and His words. Nothing more needs to be said for our salvation and our full redemption. He is Truth. He said of Himself, "I am the way, the truth, and the life: no man cometh unto the Father but by me" — the eternal way, the eternal truth, the eternal life, and furthermore, the *only way*, the *only truth*, and the *only life!* (See John 14:6.)

God's Word, being eternal, is also ongoing and perpetual. A wonderful example of this is when God said, "Let there be light." He set into motion an unending chain of "light bursts" — *"Let there be light...light...light...light...light"* — unending in time and space. The words He spoke are still going out. Light is still being shined into places of darkness. Light is still filling the dark souls of men and women.

The Bible also tells us that all things are upheld by God's Word. He does not create and then say to His creation, "Now fend for yourself." He upholds what He creates...and upholds it...and upholds it...and upholds it. When God speaks, we can stand on His Word forever and know for certain He will be faithful to perform what He has spoken.

However, God is not through speaking to His people! His written Word is the foundation upon which we build our lives, but He also speaks to us by His Spirit. If we are truly worshippers of Him, our eyes on Jesus and our ears constantly listening to the still small voice of the Holy Spirit within us, we know that He is speaking to us continuously throughout our day, leading us and guiding us and giving us revelation, wisdom, and even insight into the future. He is also speaking to us today as individuals, as churches, and as the Church at large through words of prophecy.

The problem with many people is that they experience a "word" from the Lord and then go off by themselves to build an entire movement on one word. The prophetic word of God's wisdom and knowledge is ongoing and must be continually weighed in light of the Holy Scriptures. God will not speak today in contradiction to what He has written in His Word. Nevertheless, we have to keep our spiritual ears wide open to catch the daily and seasonal leading of the Holy Spirit as well as the prophetic directions and instructions to the body of Christ at large. God wants to talk to His people!

THE PROGRESSIVE WORD

To the intent that now unto the principalities and powers in heavenly places might be known by the church the manifold wisdom of God.

EPHESIANS 3:10

57

In this verse of Scripture, we see in one little word another great truth about God's Word. Underscore that word *now*. What was hidden before is *now* revealed. God's Word is also progressive. He does not reveal all truth or all of our lives to us all at once, but in stages and increments as we need to know and can handle it. The apostle Paul is keenly aware that God is the master of all timing and that His timing is perfect. He has a particular time for the release of all things toward those who love Him and worship Him. Solomon expressed this truth in these famous words from the book of Ecclesiastes:

To every thing there is a season, and a time to every purpose under the heaven:

A time to be born, and a time to die; a time to plant, and a time to pluck up that which is planted;

A time to kill, and a time to heal; a time to break down, and a time to build up;

A time to weep, and a time to laugh; a time to mourn, and a time to dance;

A time to cast away stones, and a time to gather stones together; a time to embrace, and a time to refrain from embracing;

A time to get, and a time to lose; a time to keep, and a time to cast away;

A time to rend, and a time to sew; a time to keep silence, and a time to speak;

A time to love, and a time to hate; a time of war, and a time of peace...

He hath made every thing beautiful in his time: also he hath set the world in their heart, so that no man can find out the work that God maketh from the beginning to the end.

ECCLESIASTES 3:1-8,11

There is a perfect time for every detail of your life, and God knows those times. When you praise and worship Him faithfully and sincerely, He will reveal the times and seasons of your life, but God's Word to you is always *progressive*. It is planted in your heart, it buds, it grows, it develops, and finally it yields a harvest in your life. In His mercy and understanding, God gives you only as much revelation as you can stand at that time of your life.

If He had told you ten years ago what He would have you doing now, your mind would have been blown. You would have run! You wouldn't have been ready for all that lay ahead for you. Thank God that He reveals His plan, His will, and His Word to us in progressive stages and doesn't tell us everything at once. We could not contain all revelation at once. The fact is, as much as God has done for us and through us and in us in the past, He has that much and vastly more to do for us, through us, and in us in the future. Right now, many things are a mystery to us, but we can take comfort and have the security of knowing that the blueprint has

59

been drawn. The plan is already in effect and is unfolding before us in the fullness of God's timing.

THE REVELATION OF THE LAMB

Consider for a moment the revelation of God regarding Jesus. Our first type and shadow of Him is found in the book of Genesis. After Adam and Eve sinned, they realized they were naked before God and sought to cover themselves with leaves. But we cannot cover our sin. Only God can. Thus it was the Father who walked through the Garden in the cool of the evening and found an animal, killed it, and used its skin to cover up the nakedness of Adam and Eve. God initiated the first blood sacrifice to cover the sin of man, but we were not told what kind of animal was slain.

That first nameless animal made it possible for Adam and Eve to relate to each other in a new way and to stand before God without shame. God began with the simple truth that only the shedding of innocent blood would cover the nakedness or shame of man's sinful condition.

Then Adam and Eve began to have children, and God told their first two sons, Cain and Abel, to bring Him a sacrifice. Abel brought a blood sacrifice of a lamb and Cain brought a sacrifice of grain from the ground. God rejected Cain's sacrifice and received Abel's, so Cain became jealous of Abel and killed him. (See Genesis 4:1-8.) In this story, we have the first mention of a lamb sacrificed for the sin of mankind, and God's acceptance of it.

Later, when God is delivering the children of Israel out of Egypt, He commanded the sacrifice of a lamb for the Passover. The lamb was to be a male without spot, wrinkle, or blemish. The blood of the lamb was applied to the doorpost and lintel of the doorway to the house, and that blood provided protection from death. It was at that point that man began to understand that the blood of a sacrificial lamb had a personal benefit. As believers, we apply the blood of Jesus to the door of our hearts.

Then, through the prophet Isaiah, God revealed that the Lamb was a man. The ultimate blood sacrifice would be the sacrificial death of a single, spotless, innocent, without blemish, man for the sins of the world.

> **H**e is despised and rejected of men; a man of sorrows, and acquainted with grief: and we hid as it were our faces from him; he was despised, and we esteemed him not.
>
> Surely he hath borne our griefs, and carried our sorrows: yet we did esteem him stricken, smitten of God, and afflicted.
>
> But he was wounded for our transgressions, he was bruised for our iniquities: the chastisement of our peace was upon him; and with his stripes we are healed.

All we like sheep have gone astray; we have turned every one to his own way; and the Lord hath laid on him the iniquity of us all.

He was oppressed, and he was afflicted, yet he opened not his mouth: he is brought as a lamb to the slaughter, and as a sheep before her shearers is dumb, so he openeth not his mouth.

ISAIAH 53:3-7

It was centuries later before God revealed who this man was. When John the Baptist was baptizing believers in the Jordan River, he looked out at the crowd, saw his cousin, Jesus of Nazareth, and said:

Behold the Lamb of God, which taketh away the sin of the world.

JOHN 1:29

After Jesus insisted that John baptize Him, John saw the Holy Spirit descend from heaven like a dove and rest on Him. The next day John confirmed the truth about Jesus again, "Behold the Lamb of God!" (John 1:36). In His perfect time, God revealed who the Lamb was. He held back the revelation of His Word until that precise moment in history. In the fullness of His timing, God sent forth His Son, born of a virgin.

That in the dispensation of the fulness of times he might gather together in one all things in Christ, both which are in heaven, and which are on earth; even in him.

EPHESIANS 1:10

In the fullness of times God performed His Word. Has the Lamb been slain? Yes. When Jesus died on the cross, He died as the one, true, definitive, and eternal Lamb sacrificed for the sins of the whole world. The sacrifice was made in perfect timing according to the plan of God from the beginning. As we read in Revelation, Jesus is the "Lamb slain from the foundation of the world" (Revelation 13:8). It was always God's plan that Jesus would be born and that He would be crucified, resurrected, and then ascend back to His rightful position, seated at the right hand of the Father. God knew exactly what would happen when and to whom, but He revealed these truths to His people progressively as the time was right.

BE ALERT!

Always be on the alert for God's timing. Timing is everything! Look for God to unveil something from His Word that has been hidden to you before. In your life, there are some things God couldn't tell you until now for your sake. If He had told you that some of your friends were going to leave you when you decided to live for Jesus, you might not have been able to grow up and go up to the next level of spiritual discernment and holiness. God holds everything until the time is right for you to receive it and act on it. The key to understanding and receiving God's timing, however, is found in faith.

> **F**or therein [in the gospel of Christ] *is the righteousness of God revealed from faith to faith: as it is written, The just shall live by faith.*
>
> ROMANS 1:17

We are always to walk by faith, and not by what we see and experience. Our faith tells us, "God has more to reveal to me, and He will reveal what He desires for me to understand in His perfect timing. God is doing an eternal work in me. The more I believe and grow into the likeness of Christ Jesus, the more God is going to reveal to me. And as I experience new revelations and walk in them, I am going to grow in Christ and grow strong in faith to receive even more." When we walk in faith, we see God's timing more readily.

Paul tells us in Romans 10:17 that it is God's Word that builds our faith. We must immerse ourselves in His written Word and keep our spiritual ears attuned to the voice of His Spirit by living a life of worship. Worship establishes our faith and trust in God, that "Father knows best." Then we can live our lives and carry out our calling according to His perfect timing.

5

THE FAITH
OF HIM

In whom [Christ Jesus] *we have boldness and
access with confidence by the faith of him.*

EPHESIANS 3:12

In chapter 2 of Ephesians, we explored the
workmanship of God in our lives, and that we have
this fabulous access to come boldly into the throne
room of God to obtain mercy and grace in our time
of need — anytime and anywhere. Now in this
verse of Scripture, Paul tells us that this "boldness
and access with confidence" comes only "by the
faith of him." Notice that little phrase, "of him." We
spend so much time being concerned about our
having faith *in* Jesus Christ that we often fail to
move into the deeper revelation of what it means to
have the faith *of* Jesus Christ. This is the faith with
which we worship God from the innermost core of
our being.

Do you think that Jesus Christ ever lacked faith?
Did He have any problem trusting God the Father?

Did He receive all that He asked of the Father? Did He ask only what He knew the Father desired to grant? Was His faith perfect? Our answer to these questions must be an unqualified yes!

Does Jesus Christ continue to receive all that He asks of the Father? Is His faith still perfect? And will it be perfect tomorrow, and every tomorrow on into eternity? Again, we must say yes!

Now let me ask this. Who lives in you? Who will live in you forever? Is it not this same Christ Jesus?

> I am crucified with Christ: nevertheless I live; yet not I, but Christ liveth in me: and the life which I now live in the flesh I live by the faith of the Son of God, who loved me, and gave himself for me.
>
> GALATIANS 2:20

Our boldness doesn't lie in our own faith, which can quickly melt into fear. Our confidence to move into deeper spiritual waters and take on spiritual adversaries does not rest in our own faith, but the faith of Jesus who lives and abides within us. We must continuously and diligently tap into and pull upon His bold, active, dynamic faith, a faith that never shrinks back or cowers in the face of evil. There is such a thing as holy boldness that is beyond our own courage, and that holy boldness is rooted in the faith of Jesus Christ, who dwells in us and in whom we live and move and have our being.

The same thing applies to our having access to the throne of God with confidence. Our confidence to come before the Father with our requests and petitions is confidence shed abroad in our hearts by the presence of Jesus Christ in us. Is Jesus fearful, bashful, or intimidated by coming into the presence of God the Father? Does He cower before God's throne? Is He reluctant to turn to God the Father and make known His requests? Absolutely not!

The "holy confidence" that we have to come boldly before God's throne is a confidence born of the faith of Jesus Christ in us. Because He dwells within us as our high priest, we are able to hold fast to our profession of faith and to know with confidence that He will never fail us, forsake us, or leave us. This holy confidence is the ground from which our worship flows.

Now, there is a divine move of faith that comes into our spirits that is beyond our human ability, called the *gift of faith*, identified by Paul to the Corinthians as a gift of the Holy Spirit. This gift is bestowed upon us as the Holy Spirit wills and as we require that supernatural faith to do what God has called us to do. (See 1 Corinthians 12:9.) But whether we are given the gift of faith or are walking in the everyday "faith of Him," there is one thing we can count on with certainty when it comes to the faith of Jesus Christ: His is tried and proven faith. It is a never-fail faith. It is perfect faith. And His faith is always within us for us to draw upon.

PROVEN FAITH

You will recall that when Jesus prayed in the Garden of Gethsemane, He wrestled with His own human will in those hours of agony. Finally He submitted Himself fully to the Father in His flesh and said,

> **A**bba, Father, all things are possible unto thee; take away this cup from me: nevertheless not what I will, but what thou wilt.
>
> MARK 14:36

What was it that Jesus desired to be taken from Him? What was the cup He didn't want to drink? Jesus wasn't just wrestling with the idea of going to the cross, the pain of the scourging, crown of thorns on His head, or nails driven into His hands and feet. Jesus was wrestling with becoming sin. In all of eternity, He had never known sin. In His earthly life, He had lived without sin or guile. Now the Father was asking Him to take on the sins of the whole world and to become sin. It was such a deplorable concept to Him that He prayed, "Pass this bitter cup from Me!"

In all of eternity, the Son of God had never been separated from the Father, not even for the twinkling of an eye. In His walk on earth, He had lived in complete communion with the Father, saying and doing only what the Father led Him to say and do. Now the Father was asking Him to become sin, which meant to be separated from the Father. Jesus was facing the reality of being smitten by the Father who had never shown Him anything but the most tender, abiding love. He was in agony at just the thought of facing a moment of alienation from Him.

For Jesus to pour Himself out completely — to be stripped of all glory and honor and to die as a common thief, and then to go down into the depths of the grave and face hell in our place — was an act of supreme faith. Everything Jesus faced in the hours and days after the Garden of Gethsemane required faith, total faith and nothing but faith, that the Father was going to accept the sacrifice of His life on the cross, resurrect Him from death, defeat the enemy, and unlock the gates of hell so that He might take captive what the devil had held in captivity. Furthermore, He had faith that the Father was going to fully restore Him to His position in heaven, seated at the Father's right hand.

Jesus knew the reality of what was ahead for Him. Nevertheless, He had to walk through it by faith. Through the days leading up to His trial and crucifixion, Jesus was talking His faith:

> **D**estroy this temple, and in three days I will raise it up.
>
> JOHN 2:19

> **I** lay down my life, that I might take it again.
> No man taketh it from me, but I lay it down of myself. I have power to lay it down, and I have power to take it again. This commandment have I received of my Father.
>
> JOHN 10:17-18

> **F**or as Jonas was three days and three nights in the whale's belly; so shall the Son of man be three days and three nights in the heart of the earth.
>
> MATTHEW 12:40

When it came right down to it, the cross was more terrible than even Jesus had anticipated. He cried out to the Father, "Eli, Eli, lama sabachthani?" which is to say, "My God, my God, why hast thou forsaken me?" (Matthew 27:46). There was no agony as great as being forsaken by the Father. In the end, Jesus hung His head on His shoulders and said, "It is finished."

The sun was too embarrassed to look on the death of God's only begotten Son. The ground got nervous and began to tremble. The veil of the temple was ripped from top to bottom. Law had a head-on collision with grace. The heavens themselves began to roar, and graves opened all over Jerusalem. The most awesome moment in all of history — past, present, or future — shattered time and space and echoed all the way through eternity.

The prophet Isaiah's voice from centuries past was no doubt ringing in Jesus' ears, "Surely he hath borne our griefs, and carried our sorrows: yet we did esteem him stricken, smitten of God, and afflicted" (Isaiah 53:4). Jesus was struck by His Father so that we might know what it means to have His everlasting arms wrapped around us. Jesus felt the wrath of the Father fall upon Him so that His righteousness might fall on us.

And what did Jesus have to hold on to in those darkest moments? Only one thing — His faith in God's Word. His friends vanished. They fled into the anonymity of the crowd. His disciples cowered in fear in a locked upper room. His strength ebbed from His muscles. His blood flowed from His wounds. His breath left in one long final exhale from His body. The Father turned away at the sight of the sin He became. And in the end, the only thing remaining was His faith in God's Word.

The only thing that was alive when Jesus was buried in the tomb of Joseph of Arimathea was His faith-spoken words. What God says is eternal. His Word does not end. The faith of Jesus Christ was God-faith and the words He spoke were God's words. So His faith went on believing...and believing...and speaking...and speaking. It could not end. The crucified and buried fleshly nature of Jesus didn't know that faith because His physical brain was dead. He didn't feel that faith because His physical nervous system was dead. He didn't walk or talk in that faith because His physical body was dead. But His faith was alive because His Spirit remained alive. His eternal Spirit bore His eternal faith and that faith kept believing...and believing... and believing...past His being taken down from the cross, past His being wrapped in burial cloths and spices, past His being laid in a tomb, past a stone being rolled in front of that tomb and a watch of soldiers being set to guard the tomb. His faith kept believing...and believing...and believing.

And on the third day, when the earth shook, the stone rolled from its socket, the soldiers fainted away as if they were dead, and the Son of God came walking out of that tomb in victory, it was by only one force: His faith in God's Word. Jesus went to His death and the grave and hell believing that the

Father would raise Him up. He rose from death and the grave and ascended to His Father because of His believing and the Father's response to His believing.

Jesus proved that faith in God's Word works!

THE POWER OF THE RESURRECTION

If Christ be not raised, your faith is vain.

1 CORINTHIANS 15:17

If the resurrection had not occurred, we would have no proof that faith in God's Word works, that faith in God's Word is eternal, and that faith in God's Word conquers all things. Worship would be excessively dull! But because of the resurrection, we *know* faith in God's Word works and we have something incredible and miraculous to shout about!

If in this life only we have hope in Christ, we are of all men most miserable. But now is Christ risen from the dead, and become the firstfruits of them that slept.

1 CORINTHIANS 15:19-20

How is it that we become the firstfruits of His resurrection? How is it that we can know with certainty that we will live in eternity and be raised from death to rule and reign with Jesus forever? It isn't because of who *we* are. It isn't because of our own human faith. It's because we now have Jesus Christ dwelling in us and it is by *His* faith and *His*

73

Word that we will be raised. The faith inside us today is not our faith alone, but His faith, His most excellent, proven, perfected, enduring, dynamic, eternal faith! No doubt Paul could hardly keep from shouting as he proclaimed, "In Him I live! In Him I move! In Him I have my being!" (See Acts 17:28.)

Jesus' faith has been proven. We look at the resurrection today and say, "His faith works! His faith conquers death!" It is His faith that operates inside us and will never cease to operate. It will go on believing...and believing...and believing...all the way past our moment of death to the moment of our resurrection! We would have nothing to preach if we did not have the resurrection to back us up. If Jesus hadn't risen from that grave, we would have no hope, but because He did rise, we have everlasting hope!

The power of the resurrection, of knowing Jesus is alive forevermore, gives us rock-solid confidence and faith that what God has spoken will come to pass. This revelation gave Paul the boldness and the confidence to proclaim:

> **D**eath is swallowed up in victory. O death, where is thy sting? O grave, where is thy victory?
>
> 1 CORINTHIANS 15:54-55

When you and I receive Christ Jesus as our Savior, the Spirit indwells us. The faith of Jesus

Christ is the driving force of His Spirit. It is His faith that motivates us to keep on keepin' on. It is His faith that overwhelms us with the knowledge that His Word is absolute and unchanging and eternal. It is His faith that allows us to be immovable, steadfast, abounding in the work of the Lord, knowing that Christ in us is greater than anything we might encounter on this earth. (See 1 John 4:4.)

We can worship God because of the faith of Jesus Christ in us! It is resurrection faith! It is unshakable, undeterrable faith! It is faith that abounds and overflows and conquers. It is faith that produces and continues to produce. It is faith that continues to believe...and believe...and believe because it is the faith of God Himself!

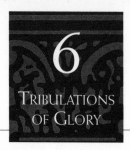

6

TRIBULATIONS OF GLORY

For ye shall go out with joy, and be led forth with peace: the mountains and the hills shall break forth before you into singing, and all the trees of the field shall clap their hands.

Instead of the thorn shall come up the fir tree, and instead of the brier shall come up the myrtle tree: and it shall be to the Lord for a name, for an everlasting sign that shall not be cut off.

ISAIAH 55:12-13

This passage of Scripture describes the life of a worshipper. Because God inhabits our praises (see Psalm 22:3), when we continually make melody in our hearts to the Lord (see Ephesians 5:19), His presence is continually with us. And when His presence is continually with us, we "shall go out with joy, and be led forth with peace." Our hearts are filled with joy and our minds kept in peace because we are safely hidden in the secret place of the Most High, warm and secure under the shadow of the Almighty (see Psalm 91:1-2) — no matter what comes our way.

FAINT NOT!

Worship sensitizes our hearts and minds to the voice of the Holy Spirit, who carefully leads us and guides us through the quagmire of darkness and evil in this life which seeks to destroy us at every turn. Worship gives us the perspective and attitude that we are not going from battle to battle and trial to trial, but from revelation to revelation and victory to victory. Maintaining an attitude of worship is vital to carrying out God's plan for our lives and overcoming the onslaught of the enemy. No one understood this better than the apostle Paul.

> *Wherefore I desire that ye faint not at my tribulations for you, which is your glory.*
> *For this cause I bow my knees unto the Father of our Lord Jesus Christ.*

EPHESIANS 3:13-14

For what cause did Paul bow his knees before the Father and worship Him? He was requesting strength and perseverance and courage for the Ephesians, that they would "faint not." The words "ye faint" are the Greek word *engkakein*, which means many things. It can mean to be frightened, discouraged, weary, or to lose hope, but the preferred meaning here is "to lose heart." Paul was concerned that when the believers saw what he had to endure for the Gospel's sake, they would lose heart, lose their passion for the kingdom, and become self-preservationists. He did not want his difficulties to frighten or discourage believers from fulfilling God's call on their lives. He wanted them to continue in steadfast prayer, reach the lost, and make disciples regardless of the trials and tribulations he endured.

When we see other believers, especially in other countries in the world today, being persecuted, tortured, and even executed because they refuse to deny Jesus as their Lord and Savior, we can lose heart and become afraid. We begin to wonder, *Could I be tortured or even die for Jesus?* Paul wants to put our hearts and minds at rest immediately by making the astounding statement that the tribulation he suffers on our behalf is for *our* glory! Only a prisoner of Christ Jesus could make such a bold proclamation and have the lifestyle and testimony to back it up.

What was Paul really trying to say? I believe he is telling us, "Look, there is more to this than meets the eye. Tribulation of this kind, which is being persecuted for the faith, brings the glory of God on the scene. In the end, the one who is going through the tribulation experiences the glory of God, the whole body of Christ experiences the glory of God, and God Himself is glorified and magnified. Moreover, when any one of us suffers by refusing to deny our Savior and Lord, it brings honor and glory to the entire Church."

The word "tribulations" can mean everything from terrible torture to extreme pressure to difficult living conditions. However, Paul's meaning of tribulations in this context is specific and definite: This is tribulation for the Gospel's sake. You are being persecuted, treated badly, or abused because you stand tall for Jesus Christ and refuse to deny Him in any way, at any time, or under any circumstances. Tribulations are definitely not something we enjoy, but they bring eternal rewards and the glory of God into our lives.

Even so, where and how does the goodness of God enter in? Surely He takes no pleasure in seeing His children suffer pain, but God's goodness does not mean that no Christian will ever suffer. And Jesus told us we would be persecuted for our faith in Him.

If the world hate you, ye know that it hated me before it hated you.

If ye were of the world, the world would love his own: but because ye are not of the world, but I have chosen you out of the world, therefore the world hateth you.

Remember the word that I said unto you, The servant is not greater than his lord. If they have persecuted me, they will also persecute you; if they have kept my saying, they will keep yours also.

But all these things will they do unto you for my name's sake, because they know not him that sent me.

JOHN 15:18-21

God's goodness toward us is that when we suffer for His name's sake, He will use that suffering to produce a great, eternal benefit for us and for the body of Christ at large. He will bring glory and honor to our lives and to the lives of all believers throughout eternity.

Paul could worship the Father in the midst of his tribulations because he knew without any doubt that what the Father called him to do, the Father equipped him to do. And what the Father equipped him to do, he could successfully accomplish. And what he successfully accomplished in obedience to the Father and by the power of the Spirit, the Father would reward. Then the Father would use what Paul did to bring about a successful, productive, reward-producing benefit in the lives of others.

Paul knew that no matter what difficulties and obstacles and trials he faced, the glory of God would be seen upon the Church because of it. He exhorted us strongly to faint not when we saw other believers go through tribulations for the Gospel's sake. This is the time when we ought to go into even higher gear to pray, study God's Word, reach the lost, and make disciples. And the Bible promises us in Galatians 6:9 that if we do not faint, at just the right time, we will reap a tremendous harvest for our faithfulness. In this case that harvest is the very glory of God!

GOING BEYOND

Let this truth sink into you — deep in you: *You can't do anything in your own strength and power that has any eternal benefit or lasting goodness.* The Father always calls us to move just beyond what we can do in our own strength and power and to trust Christ in us to do what we cannot do. He calls us to trust and then obey, knowing full well that in our own strength, we'll fail, but in Him, we will be able to do "all things through Christ which strengtheneth [us]" (Philippians 4:13). The Father always calls us to reach beyond what we can reach, to go beyond where we are, to do just a little more than we are capable of doing, and to believe something greater than we have previously believed.

When Peter and John met a lame man at the Beautiful Gate to the Temple, Peter said to him, "Silver and gold have I none." In other words, Peter said, "I don't have enough money to get you from where you are sitting right now to where God wants you to be, which is standing and praising Him inside the Temple. What I have in my own strength and ability and possessions isn't enough."

But then Peter went on to say, "But such as I have give I thee." And what did Peter have? He had the same power that raised Jesus from the dead living in him! He had the faith of Jesus surging through his being, a never-fail, eternal, always-productive faith. And when Peter relied upon what he didn't have in the natural, but what he did have in the Spirit, he said to that lame man, "In the name of Jesus Christ of Nazareth rise up and walk." (See Acts 3:1-6.)

But Peter didn't stop with bold words. He then reached down, took this man by the hand, and lifted him up. Peter did for this man what the man could not do in his own strength. The man couldn't rise on his own power, so Peter lifted him to a standing position. And as this man believed, taking into his being the power of the name of Jesus Christ, "his feet and ankle bones received strength" (Acts 3:7).

Peter moved beyond what he could do in his own ability and faith and moved into what he could do in the power of the Spirit and the name of Jesus. The lame man moved beyond anything he had ever been able to do into what he could do when he believed.

What the Father commands us to do and equips us to do is *done*. Nothing can stand in the way of the Father's will. Nothing can stop it, cut it off, keep it locked up, or cause it to be turned aside. When the Word goes forth, it doesn't return void. When we speak His Word by His faith and in His name, we will always accomplish what He wants accomplished!

Paul faced such a situation when he went to Jerusalem. He tells us that he was "bound in the spirit unto Jerusalem" and that he did not know what would happen to him there. (See Acts 20:22.) Here is Luke's account:

> **A**nd as we tarried there many days, there came down from Judaea a certain prophet, named Agabus.
>
> And when he was come unto us, he took Paul's girdle, and bound his own hands and feet, and said, Thus saith the Holy Ghost, So shall the Jews at Jerusalem bind the man that owneth this girdle, and shall deliver him into the hands of the Gentiles.
>
> And when we heard these things, both we, and they of that place, besought him not to go up to Jerusalem.
>
> Then Paul answered, What mean ye to weep and to break mine heart? for I am ready not to be bound

only, but also to die at Jerusalem for the name of the Lord Jesus.

And when he would not be persuaded, we ceased, saying, The will of the Lord be done.

ACTS 21:10-14

Ultimately, because of his visit to Jerusalem, Paul was imprisoned in Rome. He knew that Jesus helped him endure the journey that led him to Rome and the years of imprisonment which followed. He knew that what he suffered had been authorized by God and that God, by His Spirit, was equipping him to accomplish all that He commanded him to accomplish, including the strength to endure the tribulations. He saw before him a great reward for his tribulations, which were at the command of God, in the will of God, and which he was enduring by the grace of God. He wrote to Timothy:

Remember that Jesus Christ of the seed of David was raised from the dead according to my gospel:

Wherein I suffer trouble, as an evil doer, even unto bonds; but the word of God is not bound.

Therefore I endure all things for the elect's sakes, that they may also obtain the salvation which is in Christ Jesus with eternal glory.

It is a faithful saying: For if we be dead with him, we shall also live with him:

If we suffer, we shall also reign with him: if we deny him, he also will deny us:

If we believe not, yet he abideth faithful: he cannot deny himself.

Of these things put them in remembrance, charging them before the Lord that they strive not about words to no profit, but to the subverting of the hearers.

2 TIMOTHY 2:8-14

Paul saw a great reward ahead: The believers on whose behalf he was suffering were going to obtain "the salvation which is in Christ Jesus with eternal glory" (v. 10). And he saw that he would be reigning with Jesus for eternity, crowned with His righteousness forever. At the end of his life, when he knew it was time for his life on earth to end, he wrote:

For I am now ready to be offered, and the time of my departure is at hand.

I have fought a good fight, I have finished my course, I have kept the faith:

Henceforth there is laid up for me a crown of righteousness, which the Lord, the righteous judge, shall give me at that day: and not to me only, but unto all them also that love his appearing.

2 TIMOTHY 4:6-8

Paul saw a crown of righteousness going to all those who believed as he did, those who were eagerly awaiting the Lord's return. He saw a reward for his faith and obedience, and it was a reward that benefited not only himself but the Ephesians. His tribulations were also for their glory.

IT'S NOT ABOUT YOU

Your tribulations for the Gospel's sake are not only for you. They are not only so you can grow in faith and experience more of the promises of God in your life. They are not only so you can defeat the enemy and walk in victory. What you do in being a prisoner of the Lord Jesus Christ is also for the benefit of others. Your works impact people. What you say touches them. As Paul said in 2 Timothy 2:14, it is for "the subverting of the hearers." It is so that all arguments and unprofitable words and silly quarrels can be put to rest once and for all. Our tribulations for Christ Jesus have a higher purpose and a more noble cause: They bring glory to God and to His Church.

Even though we may suffer, be in bonds, or even die, the Word of God is not bound by our circumstances. It continues to speak...and to speak...and to speak about the glory of God. It continues to speak of our salvation in Jesus Christ, our eternal life in Him, our reign with Him, and our bringing glory to Him. No matter how we may suffer, the Word of

God in us continues to go forth to prosper, to bless, to produce, and to bring eternal life.

Have you ever stopped to think about all that Paul wrote from prison? Not only did he write the letter to the Ephesians, but also the epistles to the Philippians and Colossians, as well as pastoral letters to Timothy (1 and 2 Timothy), Titus, and Philemon. Furthermore, it was while Paul was in prison that Luke went about doing all of the research he did to write an "orderly account" to Theophilus, which we know as the gospel of Luke and the book of Acts. How much less would the Church know if Paul had not suffered on our behalf?

If Paul had not been imprisoned and undergone tribulations, would we have had the great teaching and encouragement of these books? Furthermore, his imprisonment and suffering bring authenticity to his words, cause them to ring true in the heart, and convict believers to stand strong in Jesus Christ as he did.

> I would that ye should understand, brethren, that the things which happened unto me have fallen out rather unto the furtherance of the gospel;
>
> So that my bonds in Christ are manifest in all the palace, and in all other places;
>
> And many of the brethren in the Lord, waxing confident by my bonds, are much more bold to speak the word without fear.

PHILIPPIANS 1:12-14

God hath not given us the spirit of fear; but of power, and of love, and of a sound mind.

Be not thou therefore ashamed of the testimony of our Lord, nor of me his prisoner: but be thou partaker of the afflictions of the gospel according to the power of God:

Who hath saved us, and called us with an holy calling, not according to our works, but according to his own purpose and grace, which was given us in Christ Jesus before the world began.

2 TIMOTHY 1:7-9

Paul's suffering was indeed for the glory of the believers who read his letters, in his time and today. What a great ongoing reward is Paul's! Have you ever stopped to think that he is still drawing reward from what you and I do in response to the truth we read in his epistles? His reward goes on and on. Why? Because it is an eternal reward from the Father for his obedience and trust in doing the Father's work by the Father's power!

Even in our suffering and tribulation, God makes certain that His Word goes forth to produce the result for which He sent it. Our part is to trust, to believe, and to obey. God's part is to use our trust and our efforts and our faith to do what He desires to do. In Paul's case, He brought forth a lasting work in the hearts of men and women around the world, not only in his generation, but in the generations following.

Paul set a remarkable, supernatural example for us, and that's the greatest point to be made here. He did not do what he did in his own strength, and neither can we. He bowed his knees to the Father to receive divine ability and capacity to run the race set before him. Thank God, the same strength and courage and perseverance and grace that Paul received from God are available to us. So now it is our turn to bow our knees to the Father!

When our families and neighbors and associates at work see us go through tribulations trusting and believing God, acting on His Word, and worshipping Him in the midst of the greatest persecution and ridicule, our rewards will continue for generations. But more than that, our tribulations glorify God and reflect glory upon the body of Christ at large. Most important, as a result many will come to know the Lord. There is no more powerful witness to this perishing, lost generation than a believer who brings glory to God and His Church through tribulations for the Gospel's sake.

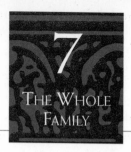

For this cause I bow my knees unto the Father of
our Lord Jesus Christ,
Of whom the whole family in heaven and earth
is named.

EPHESIANS 3:14-15

God will eventually pull everything He has
created together under one name — the name of
Jesus. Heaven. Earth. The whole family. As believers
in Christ Jesus, we are to worship God with an
awareness of that reality. In writing to the Ephesians
about the "whole family" of God, Paul is making
reference to the "holy convocation" that awaits us in
eternity. This holy convocation is God's master plan
for all things that were, are, and ever will be. It is also
the culmination of His master plan for the Church.

THE CHURCH OF THE FIRSTBORN

For ye are not come unto the mount that might be
touched, and that burned with fire, nor unto blackness,
and darkness, and tempest,

And the sound of a trumpet, and the voice of words; which voice they that heard intreated that the word should not be spoken to them any more...

But ye are come unto mount Sion, and unto the city of the living God, the heavenly Jerusalem, and to an innumerable company of angels,

To the general assembly and church of the firstborn, which are written in heaven, and to God the Judge of all, and to the spirits of just men made perfect.

HEBREWS 12:18-19,22-23

The Church is so much bigger than most Christians think it is! We tend to think of "church" as the building we go to on Sundays or the body of believers with whom we meet on a regular basis. If we think bigger, we think the whole Church is comprised of believers between California and New York, and maybe a few in Alaska and Hawaii. In our arrogance, we think "our few and no more" make up the Church. But the "church of the firstborn" is bigger than America, much bigger! It is the Church of the whole world throughout time. Any person who has bowed, is bowing, or will bow to the name of Jesus is part of "the general assembly and church of the firstborn, which are written in heaven...the spirits of just men made perfect" (Hebrews 12:23).

The Church is bigger than today, encompassing yesterday and tomorrow as well — all of then and all of forevermore. When God sees the Church, He sees the Church that is and was and will be. He sees people who are going to believe in Christ Jesus who haven't even been born yet. God always sees things from the perspective of eternity.

God knows precisely what He needs from you today that will have an impact on a believer whom you will never meet on this earth, who lives halfway around the world, but who will be blessed by what you do and enabled to bless others in his own ministry. He knows precisely what He wants you to say today that will be repeated down through the generations to touch someone who is born a century from now, should He tarry. He knows how to use your whole life — your prayers and your giving and your words and your deeds — to bless people you don't know and will never know in this life, but who are people with whom you will live forever.

It is because God sees everything from an eternal perspective that we can say things happen now that were predestined before the foundation of the world. It is because God sees all of eternity that we can know that the Lamb was slain from the foundation of the world on our behalf. God fixes His purposes in eternity and He manifests His purposes in time.

When you are going through trouble and times of tribulation, you can know with certainty that God is going to bring you through that experience and that He is going to work all things together for your good. Why? Because He sees your eternal future. Your eternal future is with Him, and that means your eternal future is not only good, but it is glorious beyond your imagination! As part of the "church of the firstborn," you are viewed in light of eternity at all times, and God wants you to view yourself that way too.

THE GREATEST WORSHIP EVER

The greatest worship experience you will ever have isn't going to happen in your local church next Sunday, no matter how great that worship experience may be. God has an even greater one planned in eternity. It is a worship service in which the whole family is gathered — not only Jews and Gentiles worshipping together, and not just several denominations worshipping together. It will be a time when you join with believers from every background and corner of this world, from every generation past and every generation future. All of us will be worshipping God around His throne with the innumerable host of angels. In one accord we will cry, "Holy, holy, holy" to our Father.

Anytime we begin to worship the Father, we need to catch a glimpse of the heavenly convocation that is also worshipping Him. We need to see with spiritual eyes that we are worshipping God with a vast congregation of saints, that we are "compassed about with so great a cloud of witnesses" (Hebrews 12:1). We need to see with spiritual eyes that we are worshipping God in the midst of countless angels — the very host of heaven — who join their voices with ours in crying, "Thou art worthy."

And when he had taken the book, the four beasts and four and twenty elders fell down before the Lamb, having every one of them harps, and golden vials full of odours, which are the prayers of saints.

And they sung a new song, saying, Thou art worthy to take the book, and to open the seals thereof: for thou wast slain, and hast redeemed us to God by thy blood out of every kindred, and tongue, and people, and nation;

And hast made us unto our God kings and priests: and we shall reign on the earth.

And I beheld, and I heard the voice of many angels round about the throne and the beasts and the elders: and the number of them was ten thousand times ten thousand, and thousands of thousands;

Saying with a loud voice, Worthy is the Lamb that was slain to receive power, and riches, and wisdom, and strength, and honour, and glory, and blessing.

And every creature which is in heaven, and on the earth, and under the earth, and such as are in the sea, and all that are in them, heard I saying, Blessing, and honour, and glory, and power, be unto him that sitteth upon the throne, and unto the Lamb for ever and ever.

REVELATION 5:8-13

John writes in Revelation that our voices join those who are singing a "new song" to the Lamb with the angels and the elders. When we worship, all of those in heaven fall down at His feet and join our worship, crying a loud "Amen!" to every word of praise and worship that we utter.

Have you ever been in a house of prayer or in your home, worshipping the Lord by yourself, when you suddenly felt deep in your spirit, *I'm not alone.* You were right! You are never alone in your worship of the Father. You are just one voice of the whole family of believers on heaven and earth that have worshipped, are worshipping, and will worship Him forever. Your voice not only joins the vast host of saints and angels in heaven, but their voices join yours here on earth.

Are you aware that when you begin to worship the Lord in the quiet of your house, angels move into your house and worship Him right along with you? The Bible tells us that the angels of the Lord encamp around those who worship the Lord. The angels don't just sit there in their worship. They worship along with you. Their job is to deliver you. David wrote,

> *The angel of the Lord encampeth round about them that fear him, and delivereth them.*
>
> PSALM 34:7

The word "fear" encompasses several realms of thought and emotion. It means a deep love, an abiding reverence, and the utmost respect for the absolute authority and sovereign rule of the Creator God. This abiding respect includes a holy fear of a God whose holiness and righteousness will destroy evil as well as give life. We definitely do not want to be standing in a place of opposition to our God! But the great news is, when we stand with God and our hearts are pure before Him, He will take care of the evil that attempts to destroy us. To fear God means to worship Him fervently, and fervent worship releases the angels to deliver us and put us into a position to receive the full blessings and provision of the Lord.

Open your spiritual eyes today as you worship the Lord! See the great host of angels camping about you, strong and glorious and countless in number. See the great host of saints, some who are the Old Testament saints who died in faith, not yet having seen the promise of Jesus Christ yet embracing Him from afar. See those who come from denominations other than yours, who perhaps don't know hymn number 856! See believers who are from other centuries, who are of other colors, customs, and cultures. You are going to have to take off the blinders of your little prejudices and biases and doctrines and organizations and movements to see your whole family!

The worship of the Lord is for the whole family together, not the family separated into little clique groups gathered in this corner and that corner, some standing, some sitting, and others on their faces. No — the whole family is united and inter-mingled as one family, in heaven and earth, and all are bowing before the Lord. God desires for us to be one because it is only in a unified body that His power can be released. It is only when we see ourselves bonded together under the authority of the divine Chief Executive Officer, who gives us a vision for this "mystery corporation" called the Church, that we can begin to experience the full-ness of the Holy Spirit's power in our midst. Paul is adamant about unity.

> There is one body, and one Spirit, even as ye are called in one hope of your calling;
> One Lord, one faith, one baptism,
> One God and Father of all, who is above all, and through all, and in you all.

EPHESIANS 4:4-6

When we come together with the whole family, we are in a position to receive a greater blessing from God. There are blessings that are not poured out by God on individuals, but on the whole family. It is only as we are fully a part of that whole family and see ourselves as being in fellowship with the whole family that we can receive those blessings.

The fact is, you can never really worship God all by yourself. Others in the family are always worshipping with you, even if you cannot see them and aren't aware of them. So from now on, whether you are worshipping the Lord with other brothers and sisters in Christ Jesus or are worshipping alone in your living room, worship with the whole family! Worship with the heavenly host. Worship Him with an awareness that He is Lord of *all*.

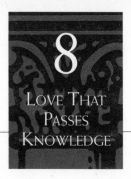

8

LOVE THAT PASSES KNOWLEDGE

Many Christians today stand like stones or merely go through the motions during worship because they live beneath their privileges as children of God, and the greatest privilege of being God's child is receiving His love and joy. God's unconditional love and exceeding great joy are the security and strength we must have to fulfill His plan for our lives and enjoy it.

We must draw upon the warmth and comfort of our most valuable friend and resource, the Holy Spirit who lives within us. The Spirit is always available to pump the Father's unconditional love, strength, and truth into the part of us that counts the most — our inner man.

MIGHT BY HIS SPIRIT

For this cause I bow my knees unto the Father of our Lord Jesus Christ,

*Of whom the whole family in heaven and earth
is named,*

*That he would grant you, according to the riches
of his glory, to be strengthened with might by his
Spirit in the inner man.*

EPHESIANS 3:14-16

I first want you to notice that little phrase, "in the inner man." Paul did not say in the inner *child,* but the inner *man.* Paul was expecting the Ephesians to mature and to grow up in Jesus Christ. So many believers today see themselves as weak spiritually, and many of them are weak. Why? They have not grown up in Christ because they are still living as malnourished and underdeveloped children *on the inside.* They have not received the "riches of his glory," nor have they been "strengthened with might" by the Holy Spirit.

The Greek word translated "strengthened" is very interesting. It is the word *krataiootheenai,* which means an infusion of that which invigorates and energizes — in this case "might" or *dunamis,* the energy to do work or the enabling power, which flows right out of the riches of God's glory. This verse paints a vivid and powerful picture in our minds of the Holy Spirit flooding our spirits with His ability and wisdom. We must understand that the Holy Spirit lives in us to empower us to succeed at whatever God calls us to do.

The heir, as long as he is a child, differeth nothing from a servant, though he be lord of all;

But is under tutors and governors until the time appointed of the father.

GALATIANS 4:1-2

A baby boy may be born to a king, but that little boy, even though he is a prince destined for a throne, is still going to be told what to do, where to go, and how to live — just as if he were a maid or a butler. Even though we are destined to rule and reign with Jesus Christ as joint heirs, many of us have not yet obtained the maturity to receive our inheritance. We still rely heavily on the pastor or a friend in the Lord to guide us and correct us instead of forming an intimate relationship with the Father ourselves. We continue to require other believers to tell us what to do, where to go, and how to live, and we live as little children, weak and ineffectual. The only thing that will enable us to grow up in Christ is to tap into the power of the Holy Spirit within.

The problem is, many believers are only desiring outer strength — a strength that can be measured in terms of things and possessions and titles and associations and power and prestige — and even biceps! I'm not interested in teaching you how to get another designer tie or how to get a house with a three-car garage instead of a two-car garage.

Things we own are not a proof of faith or of spiritual strength. I'm not against prosperity, and I believe in being healthy and blessed, but let me also assure you that the people listed in Hebrews 11 — the great giants of faith — didn't prove their faith by the things they acquired or by how much they possessed at the time of their death!

No chapter in the Bible defines faith more than Hebrews 11, and when we read through that chapter, we find that Noah lost everything that he couldn't take into the ark and Abraham lived in tents and died looking for but never seeing a "city which hath foundations, whose builder and maker is God" (Hebrews 11:7-10).

We find that the mighty in faith — people such as Gideon, Barak, Samson, Jephtha, David, Samuel, and the prophets — "wandered about in sheepskins and goatskins; being destitute, afflicted, tormented" and that they "wandered in deserts, and in mountains, and in dens and caves of the earth" (Hebrews 11:37-38). The mighty in faith went through all kinds of crises and turmoil. Some were tortured, others were mocked and scourged, others suffered bonds and imprisonment, some were stoned and sawn asunder and slain with the sword. (See Hebrews 11:35-37.) So why do we in the Church today evaluate faith on the basis of temporal things and temporal power? God has something far greater in mind for us! He wants us to be strong in the inner man.

I'm not saying to give up things. Thank God He has given you things! Things can be wonderful, but ultimately, they are no big deal. Everybody's got things. But that isn't where real strength lies. Things rust, rot, wear out, get eaten by moths, and are destroyed by fire and tornadoes and hurricanes and floods. The same goes for prestige, fame, and worldly power. Politicians get elected and then get defeated. A person can be number one today and forgotten tomorrow. A leader might command an army or a nation one day and not even be mentioned five years later. Nothing of this temporal world produces lasting strength. Only the Holy Spirit can give that kind of strength because only the Spirit is eternal and omnipotent.

I've never met a wino or a prostitute who got saved by having more things. I've never met a person possessed of the devil who was delivered by receiving things. I've never known a dope dealer whose life was turned around as soon as he acquired more things. The only true strength and power for changing human lives are found in the Spirit of God.

People who are strong on the inside — strong in the inner man, strong in the Spirit — can live with things or without things. Things matter very little. Things can be enjoyed, but they aren't the reason for living. Those who are strong in the Spirit live for Jesus, worshipping Him with their whole heart.

JESUS AT HOME

That Christ may dwell in your hearts by faith;
that ye, being rooted and grounded in love,
May be able to comprehend with all saints what is
the breadth, and length, and depth, and height;
And to know the love of Christ, which passeth
knowledge, that ye might be filled with all the fulness
of God.

EPHESIANS 3:17-19

Paul now reveals why he is praying for the Ephesians "to be strengthened with might by his Spirit in the inner man." It is "that Christ may dwell in your hearts by faith." The word "dwell" is the key here. It is the compound word *katoikesai*, from *oikeo*, which means "to live in as a home," and *kata*, which means "down." And this word *kata* has the sense of finality. Paul is revealing a great truth to us. Although we are saved and have asked Jesus into our hearts, when we allow the Holy Spirit to infuse us with His power, Jesus finally settles down and is completely at home in our hearts. This verse is talking about Jesus not only living in our hearts, but also feeling at home there! And the reason Jesus feels at home in us is because we are filled with and walking in the same power that He is filled with and walking in. We have allowed the Holy Spirit to fill us with Himself. Oh, that our Savior would feel as comfortable in our hearts as He is sitting with His Father in heaven!

Now, what happens when Jesus is at home in our hearts and we are infused with the power of the Holy Spirit? We become "rooted and grounded in love" (v. 17). We are securely fixed and permanently immersed in God's love. The Holy Spirit is flooding our hearts with His love (see Romans 5:5), and thus His love flows through us to others. Furthermore, in this attitude and perspective of love, we are "able to comprehend with all saints what is the breadth, and length, and depth, and height; and to know the love of Christ, which passeth knowledge" (Ephesians 3:18-19).

The love of God is not reserved for just a few "lucky" believers. It is for *all* saints. God desires for all believers to know the immense and vast love He has for His children — the breadth, length, depth, and height of His compassion toward us. No group of believers today has a lock on God's love! God's love is for black saints, white saints, Hispanic saints, Catholic saints, Baptist saints, Charismatic saints, and all saints of every description. When Jesus is at home in all of us through the power of the Holy Spirit, and we are rooted and grounded in God's love, there is no limit to what God can accomplish in the Church.

PAST KNOWING

The love of God is not something we can "know" with our mind. It is something that "passeth knowledge." It is beyond our ability to comprehend with our minds. The love of God is something we have to accept by faith in our hearts, accept as a fact of God's nature, and open our hearts to experience just as we accepted and experienced our salvation. As surely as we know we are saved by the blood of Jesus, we know we are divinely loved and eternally cherished because of the blood of Jesus.

I've traveled across the United States and halfway around the world, and I've preached in just about every kind of church you can name to many types of people, through many interpreters, in countless situations. And let me tell you, one of the hardest things to preach to this generation is the love of God. I can stare Christians right in the face and preach about the love of God and get the blankest looks!

Now, if I ask a person point-blank, "Do you believe God loves you?" that person is likely to say yes, but deep down inside, that person has doubts. They are thinking, *I hope He loves me. I've heard He loves me. I don't see how He could love me, but if you say so, maybe He loves me.* As a whole, we Christians do not fully believe that God loves us, so few of us have experienced His love.

Why are so many believers starved for the love of God? Most of us have not been taught how to accept the love of God by faith. We have been taught to obey God and that if we disobey Him, He'll chastise us. We've been taught His Word, His will, and His purpose. We have been taught seven steps to this and three steps to that and five steps to something else. But we have not been taught that God loves us and that we are to accept and receive His love by faith.

Statistical reports say that approximately one in four adult women in our nation today was molested between the ages of five and fifteen. And what is coming out now is that the number of men who were molested as boys in that same age range has grown at an alarming rate as well. Countless others who were not sexually abused have been physically abused — beaten by drunk fathers and doped-up mothers, by uncaring stepparents, and by exhausted and impatient grandparents. Those who are not physically or sexually abused have often been emotionally deprived. They have grown up in situations in which they were never fully certain they were loved, wanted, appreciated, or valued.

The Church puts up a sign and says, "All hurting people are welcome here," but when these broken, wounded, tattered, and torn people who have never fully known the unconditional love of a human being come walking through the front doors, the first thing the Church does is tell them the rules of their doctrine, the words to the hymns, and the commandments God expects them to obey. We rarely wrap our arms around the loveless, broken, wounded, and hurting and say, "God loves you and I love you."

The wounded in our midst rarely open up to bare their secrets for fear of being rejected, ostracized, and left out in the woodshed again. They may participate in the life of the Church as Sunday school teachers and choir members and worship dancers and actors in church dramas, but deep inside they are bleeding, hurting, and aching. And only one thing can ever satisfy that longing and that pain in their hearts: the unconditional, infinite, unending love of God. The breadth and length and depth and height of the love of God is what they need the most and often what they receive the least.

We bring hurting ones to Jesus and we tell them that God is their Father, but their only image of a father is linked to abuse. We say to them, "Welcome to the family," but family is where they were rejected and alienated. We teach them about authority, but authority to them is stained by pain. We tell them to submit to their mentors, but in their hearts submission is linked to a total lack of value.

Those who have been wounded by their fathers, whether sexually, physically, or emotionally, are people who are afraid of their heavenly Father. They fear His presence. They fear His knowing their innermost thoughts. They fear He will never love them. They fear they will never be good enough, clean enough, talented enough, or valuable enough to be accepted by Him in His kingdom.

Anytime a child doesn't know that his father loves him, he is destined to be dysfunctional. That's why Paul said, "I pray that you might know the love of Christ." This is a love that "blows the mind" because it's beyond anything we can *know*. It cannot be compared to anything we grew up with, experienced in the past, are married to, or have given birth to. The love that God has for us is infinitely pure, infinitely accepting, infinitely patient and kind, infinitely generous, infinitely *more* than any other kind of love. It's so high, you can't get over it. It's so low, you can't get under it. It's so wide, you can't go around it. It's so deep, you can never get to the bottom of it. And what you cannot fathom with your mind, you can never exhaust!

The love of God must be accepted by faith. How do we do that? In the same way we accept the salvation of our souls by faith. We choose to believe with our will that God is true to His Word and that His nature is love and that when we are in Christ, we are His beloved. (See Ephesians 1:6.) Then we look at the cross. The death of Jesus Christ on the cross is the ultimate expression of God's love. He was God's only begotten Son! And to show us how much He loved us, God required that His Son open His arms on the cross as an open invitation of embrace, saying, "This is how much I love you." John tells us this in the most famous verse in all the Bible:

> **F**or God so loved the world, that he gave his only begotten Son, that whosoever believeth in him should not perish, but have everlasting life.
>
> JOHN 3:16

Paul expressed it this way:

> **G**od commendeth his love toward us, in that, while we were yet sinners, Christ died for us.
>
> ROMANS 5:8

In receiving Christ as our Savior, we receive the full expression of God's love toward us. There is absolutely nothing that we have to do — or which we can do — to earn God's love. God loves us through Jesus Christ. He loves us because He desires and chooses to love us. We experience His love only as we accept all that Jesus Christ did for us on the cross and open our hearts to Him in faith. As John also wrote, "We love him, because he first loved us" (1 John 4:19). He gave Himself an offering and a sacrifice for us.

And we have known and believed the love that God hath to us. God is love; and he that dwelleth in love dwelleth in God, and God in him.

1 JOHN 4:16

The love of God is not something we can acquire simply by knowing. We must experience it, which is made possible by the indwelling of the Holy Spirit. Paul wrote this to the Romans: "The love of God is shed abroad in our hearts by the Holy Ghost which is given unto us" (Romans 5:5). It is the Holy Spirit who convinces us of God's love, infuses us with God's love, and who causes us to experience God's love. The fruit of the Spirit is first and foremost love. (See Galatians 5:22.)

HOW TO RECEIVE GOD'S LOVE

You will begin to feel the love of God flowing in you when you decide to accept by faith that God loves you, accepts you, and values you. You must pray, "Father, I receive Your love. I believe You love me. Help my unbelief. Help me to accept Your love. Pour out Your love on me and cause me to have the capacity to receive it. I open my heart to You. I open my life to You and I trust You to love me as I have never been loved before."

Then you need to walk in the love of God. Say to yourself a thousand times a day, if you need to, the truth of God's Word to you: "God loves me. He loves me. My heavenly Father loves me. He loves me." Pause and open your heart to Him. Let Him touch you and comfort you and hold you in His arms. And He will never withdraw His love from you if you mess up! His love is unconditional and eternal and it is His nature. He doesn't change just because you have a bad day. His love toward you goes on and on and on forever.

It is never enough to know the truth or even believe the truth. In his letters, Paul repeatedly calls for those who believe in Christ Jesus to *walk* in the truth. To walk in love is to respond to life as if we truly believe we are loved by God. How do we act when we are in love? Most people who are in love walk with their head up and shoulders back and they have a bounce in their step. Their eyes are twinkling and they have a smile on their face. They have a confidence and a glow about them that is contagious because they know they are loved. There is no dysfunction in a child who knows they are loved!

Do you know you are loved by God? Have you accepted that fact by faith? Then walk in that love! Act as if you are loved by God. "But what if I don't feel like that?" you may ask. Walk like that anyway! There are lots of times when we don't feel like the person God says we are. We are to walk as He sees us, not according to our feelings. We walk by faith and faith looks at what God says and what God promises and what God tells us. There is no place in the Bible where it says we are to walk by our feelings.

The beauty of walking by faith is that there will come that moment in time when, if we faint not, what we have been believing and acting upon will manifest. Eventually we will begin to experience and feel God's love for us. And it is the love of God that heals us, bathes us, washes us, cleanses us, restores us, builds us up, and makes us whole. The love of God is critically important for us to experience if we truly are to have an identity as His son or daughter.

God's love is what heals us from the inside out and enables us to enter into healthy, whole relationships. His love destroys and dispels any desperate clinging to another person or need to manipulate others. So many believers today are basing their relationships upon the idea that a spouse will heal and restore everything inside them. No human being is capable of doing that! Only the Lord can heal certain things in us by His love.

Those who know God's love and are walking in God's love are not desperate people, turning to this one and that one in hopes that someone will value them and love them. They aren't people who are continually changing their hairstyles and clothes in hopes of attracting someone who will love them. They aren't desperate for attention or continually questioning whether they are acceptable in the eyes of others. To know the love of Christ is to know the most awesome love a person can ever know. It is to be forever satisfied and content and fulfilled.

Always remember: God's love for you never fails. It "beareth all things, believeth all things, hopeth all things, endureth all things" (1 Corinthians 13:7). God never gives up on you. He bears with you in times when you are serving Him with your whole heart and times when you aren't. He believes the highest and best for you, even when you can't believe that for yourself. He hopes, with the assurance of eternity, that you will be blessed beyond measure, even when you are so swallowed up by circumstances that you don't feel hope. He endures all things, even your doubts and rejection of Him. God's love is kind. It is patient. It is *perfect*. (See 1 Corinthians 13.)

Those who have truly experienced God's love and who walk in the full understanding of God's love are those who never have to be enticed to worship. They don't need professional praise singers to get them to enter into praise and worship before the Father. They have a fountain of love inside of them that bubbles up continually and never runs dry because they walk in the full assurance that the Father will never reject them, leave them, bring up their past, or scorn them. They are filled with His love and overflowing with praise and worship to Him at all times.

9

A FINAL CALL
TO WORSHIP

Paul closes his prayer for the Ephesians with praise
to God:

> **N**ow unto him that is able to do exceeding
> abundantly above all that we ask or think, according
> to the power that worketh in us,
> Unto him be glory in the church by Christ Jesus
> throughout all ages, world without end. Amen.
>
> EPHESIANS 3:20-21

"Now unto him." "Him" refers to our God, who
loves us infinitely and is omnipotent with all might
and strength. Paul says that He is "able to do
exceeding abundantly above all that we ask or
think," and the Greek language here indicates that
the ability of our God transcends and goes far
beyond the highest measure we could imagine.
This is one of those phrases in Scripture where we
intensely search for some English word that might
even come close to portraying the fullness of God's

power. In the end, the translators of the *King James Version* settled for "exceeding abundantly."

God wants us to know that He is *able*. No matter what we face in life, He is able to handle it — and He is able to empower us to handle it. Now, we all know that it is nice to have someone who loves us, but if they aren't able, it's a bad situation! If God only loved us and didn't have power, we might be encouraged, but we would fail. On the other hand, if God only had power and didn't love us, we might be delivered, but we would feel crushed in our spirits. Thank God that is not the reality here! With both the love and strength of God together, we have an unbeatable combination.

The might of the Spirit is beyond our comprehension. None of us can fathom the power of God in creating this entire universe and upholding it moment to moment. The love of Christ is beyond our knowing. None of us can ever fully fathom why God loves us, how much God loves us, or the countless manifestations of God's love toward us. Put them together — might and love — and there simply is no way we can take in all that truth and ecstasy! So how do we experience the full expression of God's might and love? Paul says this vast resource of God's love and might is experienced by

us "according to the power that worketh in us"
(Ephesians 3:20).

ACCORDING TO...

Here we have that word "according" again! In the first two chapters of Ephesians, "according" always referred to something God did. But in this verse in chapter 3, Paul is telling us that the degree to which we experience God and the success we achieve as Christians depends on the degree to which *we allow* the Spirit of God to fill us, empower us, illuminate us, and move us. And the way we allow the Spirit of God to transform us in this manner is to be a worshipper of God, to be completely His.

When we worship God, we open the floodgates of God's love and might toward us. We begin to understand the unsearchable riches of the wealth He has given us in Christ Jesus. We begin to understand how to walk the walk He has placed before us. We start knowing things that are unknowable, doing things that are not doable, having things that are not haveable, reaching things that are unreachable, touching things that are untouchable — according to His power that worketh in us. We can *know* He is able and loves us exceeding abundantly, beyond our imagination and reason, as we allow His Spirit free reign in our hearts and minds.

Paul wrote to Timothy that God had not given us the spirit of fear — He did not give us a spirit of doubt, low self-esteem, or weakness — but rather, *love* and *power* and a *sound mind*. (See 2 Timothy 1:7.) He gave us His love, His power, and His wisdom. How? By the Holy Spirit. When Jesus was just about to return to heaven, He told His disciples not to go anywhere or do anything until they had received the power of the Holy Spirit.

> **A**nd, behold, I send the promise of my Father upon you: but tarry ye in the city of Jerusalem, until ye be endued with power from on high.
>
> LUKE 24:49

Let's read Luke's account of this in the book of Acts:

> **T**he former treatise have I made, O Theophilus, of all that Jesus began both to do and teach,
>
> Until the day in which he was taken up, after that he through the Holy Ghost had given commandments unto the apostles whom he had chosen:
>
> To whom also he shewed himself alive after his passion by many infallible proofs, being seen of them forty days, and speaking of the things pertaining to the kingdom of God:
>
> And, being assembled together with them, commanded them that they should not depart from Jerusalem, but

wait for the promise of the Father, which, saith he, ye have heard of me.

For John truly baptized with water; but ye shall be baptized with the Holy Ghost not many days hence.

When they therefore were come together, they asked of him, saying, Lord, wilt thou at this time restore again the kingdom to Israel?

And he said unto them, It is not for you to know the times or the seasons, which the Father hath put in his own power.

But ye shall receive power, after that the Holy Ghost is come upon you: and ye shall be witnesses unto me both in Jerusalem, and in all Judaea, and in Samaria, and unto the uttermost part of the earth.

And when he had spoken these things, while they beheld, he was taken up; and a cloud received him out of their sight.

ACTS 1:1-9

Of the hundreds of disciples who heard and saw Jesus at this time, only 120 remained to receive the power of the Holy Spirit in the upper room in Jerusalem, but what a time those 120 saints had! On the Day of Pentecost, they also experienced the fullness of the power that had calmed the stormy seas, cast a legion of demons from a raging man, and raised Lazarus from the dead.

When Jesus, true to His Word, poured out the Holy Ghost all over them, a mighty, rushing wind swept through the upper room, tongues of fire appeared on their heads, and fiery tongues of every kindred and tribe came gushing out of their innermost being. They hit the streets and Peter, who days before had denied the Lord three times and proved himself to be a base coward, preached a passionate, religion-busting, tradition-breaking, Holy Ghost message. In one day the same power that resurrected Jesus from the dead swept through the streets of Jerusalem and brought three thousand people into the kingdom of God! (See Acts 2.)

This is what God wants us to be walking in right now, this power to witness boldly and bring in a mighty harvest of souls, but it is "according to the power that worketh in us." According to... According to... We must have the power of the Holy Spirit operating full force and without hindrance in our lives to fulfill the mandate God has given us in these last days.

AMEN

Unto him be glory in the church by Christ Jesus throughout all ages, world without end. Amen.

EPHESIANS 3:21

How often do we hear the saints cry, "All the glory goes to God!" and "Glory to God!" But do we really understand there is no other place for the glory but on God, in God, through God, and on whomever God chooses to bestow it? The glory belongs exclusively to Him. Worshippers have that settled in their minds and hearts, and if an issue or situation arises where they are tempted to give glory elsewhere, they settle it again. God alone gets the glory.

The phrase "throughout all ages, world without end" actually means "all the generations of all the ages." There is no moment in time when God does not receive glory! The fact that we must remember is that He does not receive glory from the world, the secular media, the movies, or unbelievers in general. God receives glory from us, His Church. We have that privilege, honor, and responsibility throughout eternity — and if we haven't begun, we can begin right now!

If you have not set your will to be a worshipper of God, a prisoner of the Lord Jesus Christ, don't waste another minute! Make that decision now. Allow the magnificent power of the Holy Spirit to fully inhabit your life and endue you with God's ability and love. Let Him transform you to reach higher and higher heights of joy and revelation in Christ Jesus.

Paul ends his prayer with the simple word "Amen." "Amen" is another word we say all the time and never think about what it means. But I can tell you that if we did, we'd keep our mouths shut a whole lot more than we do! You see, "amen" means that everything we just declared is absolutely, unequivocally true. There is no arguing with a statement that has an "amen" at the end of it! Therefore, when Paul says "amen," he means, "Everything you have just read is true. Don't even think about doubting it. The Word of God will stand forever, and you can build your life upon it without the slightest hesitation or anxious thought."

IN SPIRIT AND IN TRUTH

The last amen truth I want to put you in remembrance of about our worship is what Jesus told the precious Samaritan woman at the well:

> The hour is coming, and now is, when the true worshipers will worship the Father in spirit and truth; for the Father is seeking such to worship Him.
> God is Spirit, and those who worship Him must worship in spirit and truth.

JOHN 4:23-24 NKJV

Did you hear that in your spirit? God is *seeking* for worshippers! He is searching the earth for those who will worship Him in spirit and in truth. When I read that my heart just leaps up and says, "Here am I, Lord! Find me! I want to worship you in spirit and in truth!"

In the fifth chapter of Ephesians, Paul admonishes the Ephesians to be filled with the Spirit (Ephesians 5:18), and the Greek language there indicates to be continually filled, every moment filling up more and more with the Spirit. He likens our being filled with the Spirit to being intoxicated with wine: "Be not drunk with wine, wherein is excess: but be filled with the Spirit" (v. 18). We are to be "under the influence" of the Spirit at all times!

When we drink of the Spirit, He energizes and activates and causes the nature of Christ to rise up in us. We do things we wouldn't normally do, say things we wouldn't normally say, and the more we drink of Him, the more we want to drink of Him. Like the wino on skid row, we can never have enough of the Spirit!

It is very obvious when a believer is drunk in the Holy Spirit. Their spiritual sight is affected, their reactions are different, their judgment reflects the wisdom of God, and the boldness they exhibit makes any complacent, lukewarm believer turn red with embarrassment. The cold, nod-to-God, Sunday morning Christian will quickly label the drunk believer a fool, but this drunken fool is what the Bible calls a fool for Christ. (See 1 Corinthians 3:18.) This is the kind of fool we all must be!

Now, a spiritual drunk with no foundation in God's Word is an accident looking for someplace to happen. On the other hand, a believer with all knowledge of the Word who is not completely under the influence of the Holy Spirit is living in a legalistic, joyless cage of religion. A real fool for Christ gives all control to the Holy Ghost and studies to show themselves approved, a workman not ashamed, rightly dividing or understanding the Word of God. (See 2 Timothy 2:15.) When we are drunk in the Spirit but grounded in God's Word, people will find out we are not such a drunken fool after all! More important, God can use us to the fullest, and we will bring glory to His name.

Being a worshipper in spirit and in truth simply means being completely dependent on the Holy Spirit and studying the Word of God continuously. We drink of the Spirit and eat of the Bread of Life; drink and eat...drink and eat...drink and eat. We come to Jesus and say, "I love You, Lord. Tell me whatever You want to tell me. Let me know what's on Your heart and mind. All I want to do is love You and be with You. Fill me up with You, Lord."

We see this when a man and woman are in love and they call each other on the phone several times a day. The conversation goes something like this:

"How are you doing?"

"Fine, how are you?"

"Just great. You want anything?"

"No, I just wanted to hear your voice and to tell you I love you."

"Oh yeah...I love you too."

That's the kind of relationship God desires from us in our worship. He longs for us to come into His presence, tell Him we love Him, and let Him know how much we delight in Him. We don't need a problem, an agenda, or even a good reason to worship Him. We are just happy to be with Him, and our very life hangs on every word He speaks. Have you ever been so happy that you just couldn't help whistling and humming and singing little songs to yourself? That's the quality of joy we are to have in our worship. Worship is not drudgery, obligation, chore, or tedious duty. It is joy and light and love and intimacy with Holy God!

Have you ever noticed how newly married couples are always trying to talk their unmarried friends into getting married? Nothing is better, nothing sweeter, nothing more enjoyable than passionate, ecstatic, joyful, blissful love! People who are in love don't go around picking fights. They don't have time or inclination for arguments. They aren't critical of others. They are floating along on "cloud nine" pretty much oblivious to the flaws, faults, and failures of others. They are so wrapped up in loving they have no room for hating.

That is the position of the believer who is lost in worship of their God. They have no room for rebellion, bitterness, anger, or hatred. They have no desire to manipulate or control others. They desire only that everybody feel the same glorious way they feel — completely and utterly consumed and ecstatic about Jesus, their Savior, their Lord, and their dearest, forever Friend.

Worship is intimacy with God. It is spending time alone with Him. It is singing to Him and talking to Him and sitting in His presence, communing with Him and listening to Him. Worship is reading the Bible and waiting for Him to give instruction and revelation and wisdom. It is praying in the Spirit and allowing Him to fill you up to overflowing with faith, love, and joy. It is delighting in His presence, completely at peace and at rest.

Our worship is loving Him more than anything else in life. Amen and Glory to God!

REFERENCES

Adam Clarke Commentary. 6 vols. Adam Clarke. *PC Study Bible.* Version 2.1J. CD-ROM. Seattle: Biblesoft, 1993-1998.

Barnes' Notes on the OT & NT. 14 vols. Albert Barnes. *PC Study Bible.* Version 2.1J. CD-ROM. Seattle: Biblesoft, 1993-1998.

The Bible Knowledge Commentary: An Exposition of the Scriptures. Dallas Seminary faculty. Editors, John F. Walvoord, Roy B. Zuck. Wheaton, IL: Victor Books. 1983-1985. Published in electronic form by Logos Research Systems Inc., 1996.

Brown, Driver, & Briggs' Definitions. Francis Brown, D.D., D. Litt., S. R. Driver, D.D., D. Litt., and Charles A. Briggs, D.D., D. Litt. *PC Study Bible.* Version 2.1J. CD-ROM. Seattle: Biblesoft, 1993-1998.

Expositor's Bible Commentary, New Testament. Frank E. Gaebelein, General Editor. J. D. Douglas, Associate Editor. Grand Rapids, MI: Zondervan Publishing House, 1976-1992.

A Greek-English Lexicon of the New Testament and Other Early Christian Literature. Walter Bauer. Second edition, revised and augmented by F. W. Gingrich, Fredrick Danker from Walter Bauer's fifth edition. Chicago and London: The University of Chicago Press, 1958.

The Greek New Testament. Editor Kurt Aland, et al. CD-ROM of the 3rd edition, corrected. Federal Republic of Germany: United Bible Societies, 1983. Published in electronic form by Logos Research Systems, Inc. 1996.

Greek (UBS) text and Hebrew (BHS) text. PC Study Bible. Version 2.1J. CD-ROM. Seattle: Biblesoft, 1993-1998.

The Hebrew-Greek Key Study Bible. Compiled and edited by Spiros Zodhiates, Th.D. World Bible Publishers, Inc., 1984, 1991.

Interlinear Bible. PC Study Bible. Version 2.1J. CD-ROM Seattle: Biblesoft, 1993-1998.

Jamieson, Fausset & Brown Commentary. 6 vols. Robert Jamieson, A. R. Fausset, and David Brown. *PC Study Bible.* Version 2.1J. CD-ROM. Seattle: Biblesoft, 1993-1998.

A Manual Grammar of the Greek New Testament. H. E. Dana, Th.D. and Julius R. Mantey. Toronto, Canada: MacMillan Publishing Company, 1927.

Matthew Henry's Commentary. 6 vols. Matthew Henry. *PC Study Bible.* Version 2.1J. CD-ROM. Seattle: Biblesoft, 1993-1998.

The New Linguistic and Exegetical Key to the Greek New Testament. Fritz Reineker, Revised version by Cleon Rogers and Cleon Rogers III. Grand Rapids, MI: Zondervan Publishing Company, 1998.

Strong's Exhaustive Concordance of the Bible. J. B. Strong. *PC Study Bible.* Version 2.1J. CD-ROM. Seattle: Biblesoft, 1993-1998.

Vincent's Word Studies in the NT. 4 vols. Marvin R. Vincent, D.D. *PC Study Bible.* Version 2.1J. CD-ROM. Seattle: Biblesoft, 1993-1998.

Wuest's Word Studies from the Greek New Testament for the English Reader. Volume One, Ephesians. Kenneth S. Wuest. Grand Rapids, MI: Wm. B. Eerdmans Publishing Company, 1953.

T. D. Jakes is the founder and senior pastor of The Potter's House church in Dallas, Texas. A highly celebrated author with several bestselling books to his credit, he frequently ministers in massive crusades and conferences across the nation. His weekly television broadcast is viewed nationally in millions of homes. Bishop Jakes lives in Dallas with his wife, Serita, and their five children.

To contact T. D. Jakes, write:
T. D. Jakes Ministries
International Communications Center
P. O. Box 210887
Dallas, Texas 75211
or visit his Web site at:
www.tdjakes.org

REFLECT THE
Radiance
OF THE MASTER

The Princess Within by Serita Ann Jakes

The Princess Within is an honest, intimate book
from Serita Jakes that helps women reflect the glory of
God as they live every day. Filled with her own stories
of struggles and triumphs, it offers tender wisdom
for every woman.

Whether you are burdened by past failures or simply
trying to draw as near to God as possible, this book will
give you the insight and strength you need.